An E₁
G

A book is food for the heart. I occasionally witness one good book changing an individual's life or even a community. Many books that I read during my youth are companions that still greatly help me in working as a public official.

This book of Pastor Ock Soo Park melts each chapter with his precious experience he gained through being with young people for the last twenty years. It is not a script written at a desk; it is based on experience he had with tens of thousands of college students he met all over the world. It didn't matter if it was a country of hot weather, cold weather, a wealthy country, or a poor country as he ran around all parts of the world without discrimination. That is why it is more valuable and touches the hearts of readers. According to the ten topics such as heart, desire, self-control, wisdom, change, and more, it shows young people of each country's anguish and agony and vividly pictures the process of them changing through open-heart conversation and raises a bond of sympathy.

As I read this book, I empirically got to know the fact that youths all around the world live inside similar anguish and difficulties, and they are able to change through sincere conversation. Especially the stories and pictures of our college students who found hope and new life as they worked as volunteers in Tanzania, Togo, Cameroon, and other remote areas of Africa truly touched my heart.

I think that such precious life experience that they gained from overseas volunteer work and activities are very precious to us. And the fact that this book well conveys such precious experiences; that is how it speaks to the phrase, "A book is food for the heart."

I heard that this book will be published in Chinese, Spanish, and more. I hope that youths from all around the world, who have fallen into agony, anguish, and who have lost the will to live, will read this book and find hope and courage.

June 2011
Minister of Culture, Sports, and Tourism of Korea
Byung-guk Chung

Letters of Recommendation

A Mind Book, Written by the "Genie," Based on His Decades of Experience, Which Is Needed in this Generation

Pardon me, but I think of Pastor Ock Soo Park as a genie. *Genie* does not mean an evil spirit, but rather it means a good existence that says, "Appear gold," and *poof!* gold appears, or "Appear silver," and *poof!* silver appears; or to an ill person he says, "Heal disease," and *poof!* the disease gets healed. In this society that's heartbreakingly divided and self-centered, Pastor Ock Soo Park goes *poof!* and stirs love in people's hearts, and moral water springs forth. He is that kind of a genie. If there are a few more people like this, the nation will become happy, people will become happy, and our country's people will be admired by the other people of the world.

The original nature of people is actually kind and good, yet we have forgotten that and have flowed to and are surrounded by a material-oriented atmosphere. Now people say, "I don't care that my neighbor is starving to death. I have money, so I can eat whatever I want. Whether others suffer from diseases and hardship, I just need to study hard and succeed."

Originally, that was not true. People who feel pain when others feel pain take them to the hospital, or at least offer them water. With this mentality and love, they can flourish. We currently are not like that. We are headed for trouble.

Pastor Ock Soo Park brings out a person's original nature. He truly is a leader. Thankfully, many young people are influenced by him, and as a result, they are living an upright life. They have developed the mentality of loving others, and they grieve together with people who are poor and undergoing difficulties.

Using his passion and experience of leading the hearts of young people for decades, he published the book titled *Navigating the Heart: Who Is Dragging You?* As they read this book, I look forward to seeing young people who used to think "Even through injustice, I've got to succeed" change and live a beautiful life of loving their deprived neighbor as themselves.

June 2011
Former President of Seoul National University
Former Prime Minister of Korea
Soo Sung Lee

Navigating the Heart

Navigating the Heart

Who Is Dragging You?

OCK SOO PARK

TATE PUBLISHING
AND ENTERPRISES, LLC

Published by Tate Publishing & Enterprises, LLC
127 E. Trade Center Terrace | Mustang, Oklahoma 73064 USA
1.888.361.9473 | www.tatepublishing.com

Tate Publishing is committed to excellence in the publishing industry. The company reflects the philosophy established by the founders, based on Psalm 68:11,
"The Lord gave the word and great was the company of those who published it."

Book design copyright © 2013 by Tate Publishing, LLC. All rights reserved.
Cover design by Rodrigo Adolfo
Interior design by Deborah Toling

Published in the United States of America

ISBN: 978-1-62854-323-0
1. Self-help / Personal Growth / General
2. Family & Relationships / General
13.09.10

Dedication

To young college students who are going through heartache due to never having learned the world of the heart and having no one to teach them.

Contents

Wisdom: True Wisdom Is Knowing

Change: The Heart Begins to Open

Preface

Many young people live having lost themselves. So instead of living on their own will, they live according to another force.

"I drink too much. I shouldn't do that."

"Would I be able to graduate college like this? I have to straighten up!"

However, they are not able to get out of it; all they can do is try to recommit themselves daily. Although they are falling into places they don't want, they cannot get out according to their wish.

"Mom, please stop! Do you think I want to live like this? I cannot control it. Every day I just want to die, so why are you torturing me too?"

There are so many students who are shouting like this. Once they fall into wrong things, they cannot get out. They simply are dragged around. They themselves, parents, or teachers cannot cut the loop and get them out.

A mother talked about the problem of her son assaulting his teacher.

"He hit a teacher? That wasn't your son."

"Yes, it was, Pastor. It was definitely my son who hit the teacher."

"No, it wasn't. It was not your son who did that!"

I explained to the mother in detail that the student did not want to do it, but it was a certain force in his heart that dragged him and made him so.

People learn many things from their birth to their death. Starting from using a spoon, they eventually learn to speak, read, and write. Once they enter school, they learn piano, tae kwon do, math, foreign languages, etc. They acquire vast knowledge, skills, and experiences. However, as they live, they have never learned about the world of the heart, which is the most important and the most necessary, and no one has taught them. Because people only know vaguely about the world of the heart, there are students that are miserable that have no reason to be miserable, and there are young people who live in sorrow that have no reason to be sad.

I discovered the stream of the heart, which is the world of the heart, in the Bible. So I established the International Youth Fellowship and taught many young people about the world of the heart through this organization. Then young people got out of game addiction, their difficult pasts, and even autism, and now they are living beautiful lives. I am very happy seeing these young people, whose hearts changed into strong hearts. I hope that this book will open the way for our young people to get out of darkness.

June 2011
Author, Ock Soo Park

Chapter 1

Heart

Like a River, There Is a Way the Heart Flows

There are many people who try to overcome addictions like playing video games or those who try to quit drinking and smoking. They try with all their strength and determination, but for the most part, they end up quitting in the middle. This is due to the fact that they do not know precisely about the world of the heart. Change in life does not come from determination and labor; it is the heart that must first be changed because like a river, there is a way the heart flows.

A Drug Addict Who Fell into His Thoughts While Eating a Piece of Spoiled Bread

There is a man named Julio who lived in New York City. He migrated to the United States at a young age with his family from South America. In America, where there is an abundance of material things, drugs are also very common. Even though the government had tirelessly tried to rid this nation of drugs, they have been unable to do so. As a result, it is very easy for students to get drugs.

From his youth, Julio had been doing drugs for almost twenty years. If you have done as much drugs as he had done, you are surely a drug addict. Julio needed drugs, but he couldn't hold a job, so he would beg and steal to get money to buy more drugs. As long as he was high, he did not feel cold, hot, or even hungry. When Julio was high, his heart felt very comfortable. Because he simply could not quit the drugs, he became homeless at a young age and ended up living and sleeping on park benches.

One day, as the drugs wore off, Julio became very, very hungry. So hungry that he started to search through the garbage for food. There were pieces of bread from discarded hamburgers that were half-eaten by children and thrown away in the park garbage. When Julio searched through the garbage, he found a piece of bread that someone had thrown away. Julio devoured it. After eating for a while, he noticed a strange taste. The taste came from one of the pieces of bread that had been spoiled. At first, he had been eating it mindlessly because he was so hungry. He only realized it was spoiled after he became full. He looked at the piece of spoiled bread in his hand and then at the pieces of the bread that had fallen to the ground and fell into the following thought:

> What am I doing right now? How did I end up becoming this kind of a person? Everyone else buys and eats bread that's fresh from the bakery, so why am I eating spoiled bread from the trash? Other people my age are married and have homes, but in my entire life, I could never actually see myself buying a home. And I will probably never get married. What kind of a woman would want to marry a drug addict? Will I even be able to have my own car one day? Will I even be able to afford a car that is a piece of junk? What will happen to me in the future?

As he looked at himself, he compared himself to others for the first time.

> Other people drive and ride in their own cars. Other people get married and come to the park for a walk with their beautiful wives and children. Other people wear nice clothes and new shoes, but what's wrong with me? I've been addicted to drugs my whole life, and I am just

going to live pitifully like this, and this is exactly how my life will end. Drugs have ruined my life.

While he was doing drugs, he never once thought about this, but for the first time in twenty years, he discovered what a failure he had become. All of a sudden, he wanted to get married. He wanted to live in a comfortable home, take his family to the park and play, and go to the bakery to buy and eat the bread that he wanted. That kind of heart erupted inside him, but when he looked at his own image, these dreams seemed intangible. It started to seem that if he continued to live the way he was living, he would end up diseased, suffering, alone on the park bench, and finally dead. At that instant, he felt fearful of death in his heart. Nevertheless, Julio continued to do drugs and was caught by the police and sent to a drug rehabilitation center.

In drug rehabilitation centers, you are not allowed to go outside for a period of time, and during that time, they train you to quit drugs. From the first day, the counselor spoke to the addicts who were mandated to be there, saying,

> Everyone, you want to quit drugs, don't you? I know you very well. Through your efforts you can never quit drugs. If you really want to quit drugs, then from this moment on, listen carefully to what I say. I have worked as a drug rehab counselor for a long time. I know how you can quit drugs.

The amazing thing was that Julio had already been to rehab twice and had heard the same counselor speak the same words, but those words had gone in one ear and out the other in the past. This time, he was able to hear what the counselor was saying. *That's right*, he thought to himself. *That is who I used to be.*

As Julio listened word for word to what the counselor said, he took a look around him. Everyone in the room was a drug addict, but no one was concentrating on what the counselor was saying. There were people who had their heads down sleeping, people who were messing around with the person sitting next to them, and people dozing off, thinking about other things. Julio had been like that before, but when he clearly discovered that he could only die from drugs in the very end, his heart began to change.

Finally, he was able to actually *hear* what the counselor was saying.

As people live—when they think that they're right, when they think that they're good, when they think that they're great, and when they think that they're smart—they are unable to listen to anything other people say. No matter what anyone says, that person will only select and listen to whatever fits his or her own heart. On the other hand, if you are a failure in life, if you are the person who has done wrong, and if you can acknowledge you are that person who is wrong, then you can actually *hear* the words another person is telling you.

And just like that, Julio was able to say, "So that's why I wasn't able to quit drugs." He was then able to concentrate on what the counselor was saying. *For twenty years, I have lived being held inside of drugs. But now, if I continue to listen like this, then I can quit drugs.* As he had such thoughts, he was able to gain strength in his heart, and just about the time when he was ready to finish his time in rehab, he was able to completely quit drugs. Now he comes to our church in Manhattan, and his life has changed.

Julio's life of wearing raggedy sneakers and sleeping on a park bench is finally over. After thinking about his future and how he would inevitably end up dying pitifully, he began to crumble within. It was because of this new position that the words of others were able to enter his heart. There are many people who try to quit playing video games, smoking, or drinking. They become determined and use all their strength to do this. While some people do accomplish this and change, most people fail along the way. This is because people do not clearly know what the world of the heart is. Change in life does not happen through determination and effort; it is the heart that must first be changed.

At This Restaurant, I Really Feel Like I Am Eating at Home

There is a college student dance team called the Righteous Stars. Last year, they received the grand prize in the two largest national dance competitions in Korea, the Ahndong Dance Competition and the Cheonan Dance Competition. They have also received prizes at other various street festivals. At the Cheonan Heungtaryung Dance Festival, the emcee said, "We have looked into the reason why the Righteous Stars are good at dancing, and we came to this conclusion: the other teams just dance, but the Righteous Stars dance joyfully." No matter how hard a person works, nothing can be compared with working joyfully. When we do things joyfully, the results are so much greater. Even when we think about quitting drugs, quitting with a hopeful, joyful heart versus quitting with our efforts and labor are vastly different. Even in a shoe store, you cannot compare just selling shoes with selling shoes with a joyful heart. If you come to know the world of the heart, it is more than "Oh, I should study hard. I should work hard." Now you are able to do everything joyfully and have fun.

There is a married couple I know that runs a restaurant in America, and they do it with such joy in their hearts. Their children are all married, and so it is just the two of them that live together. As they see the people of the neighborhood happily eating, they are satisfied. They don't have the ambition to make lots of money. When customers come, they talk with them, and when they see that the food is not enough, they give them larger portions. When the customers come to this restaurant, the heart of joy is transferred. People say to themselves, "When I eat at this restaurant, it really feels like I am eating in my own home." Everyone who comes to this restaurant has the same sentiment, so there are frequent customers, and the restaurant is doing quite well. With such a restaurant in existence, who wouldn't go there often?

A person who works with making money as their primary goal will have the heart to decrease the costs of the ingredients more and more in order to gain more profit. After a while, the food portions decrease, and the ingredients become less fresh. When the customers discover this, they no longer go to that restaurant. No matter what it may be, if you do anything for your own selfish gain, this is the outcome. Even regarding your personal studies, if you study for your own personal gain, competition becomes fierce, and relationships become difficult and superficial. If this occurs, there are many things that are lost in your heart.

Sure, if you are highly educated or extremely skilled in a particular area, you might make lots of money. But if you know the world of the heart, you could become so much happier. As a result, there would be no problems between husbands and wives. There would be no need to receive mental treatment. And there would be no need to think about suicide.

The Younger Son Who Was Filled with Confidence and Left with the Wealth

Most colleges teach students about the world of knowledge, but you cannot find an institution that teaches the world of the heart. The Bible, on the other hand, teaches about the world of the heart. The prodigal son is a particularly well-known story. There was a certain rich man who had two sons, but one day, the younger son came to his father and asked to receive the inheritance that his father was going to give him when he came of age. It makes you wonder, if the older brother was not asking for it, why was the younger brother asking for it? The younger son believed in his own ability. He believed that if he did run a business, he would succeed. That is why he was able to boldly ask his father for his portion of his father's wealth.

"Father, there's something I want to tell you."

"Okay, son, go ahead."

"Give me the portion of your wealth that is supposed to come to me."

"What? Even your older brother is not asking for anything."

"Father, I am not a little child. I want to have my own business."

"Hey, do you think doing business is that easy?"

There was an argument between the father and son, but the younger son refused to even take one step back. Since it was making the house noisy, the father just gave up and gave him the wealth. The younger son took that wealth and went to a far country, believing that if he did business with that money, he could do better than his father. He went to a new country, and everything looked amazing in his eyes. His pockets were full. On the first day, he enjoyed himself with everything he wanted and then tried to work hard on his business the following day. Because he believed in his own abilities, he thought that he would be able to do whatever he wanted. However, after spending one night at a prostitute's house, he went again the next day and the next day and the next day. He found himself returning there over and over again. First of all, if you set your foot in the house of a prostitute, it's hard to escape from it. You may think, "I am confident. I am not going to live like that." But once you find yourself in the situation, it's not so easy to simply remove yourself from it.

As time passed, the money that the younger son brought with him was being spent more and more on the prostitute. He fell deeper and deeper into that woman and wasted his entire wealth. Many times he would say, "Okay, I am not going to go there today. I'm going to plan for my business." He would make up his mind to do that, but if a prostitute were to allow that kind of man to leave, then she wouldn't be a prostitute. A prostitute knows how to melt a person's heart. Isn't that what a prostitute is? The younger son just wanted to have a little fun and then come out and run a business. But now he was unable to come out from that on his own.

Once You Fall into Something, It Is Impossible to Have Normal Logic and Actions

At the International Youth Fellowship camps, there is the Chungbuk Yeongdong pine forest where the college students camp outdoors. A river flows alongside it, and the students go rafting there. Once, I was riding on a boat with the chairman of IYF, and I told him, "Why don't you take the raft from here? I'm going into the water and will swim from here." I jumped into the river, and I didn't have any goggles on, so with my eyes closed, I put my head underwater, and I began to stroke toward the hill. After having gone for a while, I thought, *I should be at the hill by now.* But when I lifted my head out of the water, I couldn't see the hill.

"Oh, where did the hill go?" I looked around, and I was going in the opposite direction. I was going farther down the river. I once again set my direction toward the hill and stroked with my arms. After going for a while, I thought, *Oh, now I should almost be there.* But when I lifted my head once again, I was going in the opposite direction again. *This is weird. What's wrong?* I thought. I looked around, and I saw that this was the spot where two currents of water met, and there was a slight whirlpool where the water was flowing around in circles. That is where I had fallen in. *Ah, I have fallen into a whirlpool*, I thought to myself.

Even though I tried to break free from it, the strong currents held my body in, and I was just swimming around in circles. For a moment, I panicked. If you swim intensely, then you become exhausted quickly, but in order to become free from the whirlpool, I tried to swim out with all my strength. But I could not break free, and I was just growing weaker and weaker. I thought to myself, *If this continues and I become fully exhausted, then I'm just going to drown.* When I looked the other way, I saw the chairman rowing the boat and going away. I yelled out, "Chairman!" The chairman looked toward my direction. "This way! Hurry up and come here!" I yelled out. Then the chairman quickly rowed the boat back toward me. Right then I thought to myself, *One should never lose another person's heart.* What would have happened if the chairman heard me screaming but continued to leave? Because I know how to swim a little bit, I thought that the distance wasn't much of a problem for me. However, once I was caught in the whirlpool, my swimming abilities were useless.

I had fallen into a whirlpool, and the younger son, similarly, had fallen into prostitutes. Before I entered the water, just as I thought to myself, *Why can't I cross this river?* the younger son thought, *Why can't I just have fun for a day?* But he was dealing with prostitutes—women who know how to melt men's hearts. The younger son did not have any experience with this, so he fell into women, and the more he stayed with the women, his pockets became lighter and lighter.

Now I'd better start my business. I'd better break free from these women. He thought this way, but in reality, his actions could not break free. That is what it means to have fallen into something. If you fall into drinking, this means that you cannot just come out from drinking. If you fall into gambling, you cannot just come out from gambling. If you fall into drugs, you cannot just break free from drugs. If you fall into women, you cannot just break free from your addiction to women.

Nowadays, there are lots of people who have fallen into drugs, gambling, drinking, women, and even computer games. These people struggle because they are unable to break free. But these are not the only things that people fall into. Some people fall into pride, believing in the thought that they are great. Some people fall into hatred or malice. There are times when a person falls into a pit while he or she is walking. His first reaction is to panic, and then it becomes impossible for him to have logic or act calmly.

In language, we use the term *fell*. *Fell* into gambling. *Fell* into computer games. *Fell* into golf. *Fell* into women. In the same way, you may fall into a deep pit or into a deep pool of water, and you can only struggle. No matter what it may be, if you fall victim to something, your logic is shattered, and you can only wander back and forth. The younger son tried to break free from the prostitute, but ultimately, he was unable to and eventually ran out of money. That's when the woman's attitude completely changed. Before, she was so kind and willing to listen to anything he had to say. But now, very coldly, she kicked the younger son out. As the younger son came out empty-handed, he felt so empty inside. "This is what the world is. The world is such a deceitful place. How foolish I was. That woman did not love me but acted as if she did. I fell into the thought that she loved me."

The Rich Man from the Countryside Who Fell for a Prostitute from Pyeongyang and Pulled Out a Tooth for Her

There was a prostitute in Pyeongyang with a very beautiful face. Once, a rich man from the countryside fell for this prostitute. He had a euphoric time with the prostitute, but once he ran out of money, he told her that he was going to return to the countryside and bring back more money.

But the prostitute clung to him and said, "No. I cannot live without you."

"What can I do? We need the money. Let me go sell my land."

"Then I need to ask you a favor," she replied.

"What is it?" the man asked.

"Pull out one of your teeth."

"One of my teeth? What are you going to do with my tooth?"

"While you're not here, I'm going to miss you so badly. I don't think I can bear it. If you leave your tooth, I will at least be able to look at your tooth and get by."

He was so thankful that this prostitute loved him so much that he pulled out a full tooth and gave it to her. The prostitute then washed the tooth clean and wrapped it in cotton and put it into a pretty little bowl. "Until you return, I will wait for you, looking at this tooth."

This rich man from the countryside was so excited that he quickly returned to his home. Not long afterward when the rich man returned to Pyeongyang, there were rumors already going around that this prostitute was living with another man.

"That can't be!" he exclaimed and went to her house. Indeed, she was living with another man. He said to her, "I have returned." She would not even look at him. "How could you do this to me?" he asked.

"I'm a prostitute, you know," she replied.

He became so angry and said, "Give me back my tooth!"

"If you go to the storage, there is a whole basket full of teeth, so you can get yours from there," she replied.

When he opened the door and went into the storage, like she said, there was a whole basket full of teeth.

This is a prostitute whose heart flows in the direction of following money. But people fall victim to prostitutes. The younger son also felt that it was wrong to have lost all his wealth, but there was nothing he could do. And for the time being, he had to work in order to eat and live. Because he grew up as a son of a rich family, he had never done anything, so he did not know how to do anything. Then a famine came to the land. Jobs were very hard to come by. He begged door-to-door, telling people that he would work hard for them, but they could quickly see that he had no working experience at all. He was looking far and wide for a place to work, and he even went to houses and sincerely begged.

"Have you herded swine before?" someone asked.

"No, I have not, but I will work hard," he replied.

This was the only place that was available to him, so he had to at least try it. He would go out to the field and feed hundreds and hundreds of pigs every day. He was so tired from working all day long, and he was very hungry. Rather, it was the pigs that looked happy. At night, he would lie down and sleep among the pigs while the moon shone brightly. While looking at the moon, he would think about his hometown. "The same moonlight is shining upon the house where my father lives. Is he at peace? Is my older brother doing well?" Only then did regret begin to take over the younger son's heart.

"Father, Don't Make Me Your Son, Make Me One of Your Hired Servants"

He could not stay there any longer, so he determined in his heart to go home and started taking footsteps toward his father's house. He went in clothes that were rags, and he begged as he went along the way. "If I go in this image, how will Father see me, and what will he say? I was so confident in front of my father back then. What will my brother say when he sees me like this? Maybe he'll curse me, hit me, and kick me out."

As he walked like that for several days, his thoughts became more complex. He had the heart that he was no longer worthy to be his father's son, but he wanted to be kept in his father's house as a hired servant. Finally, he got closer to his father's house. Around sunset, the father was sitting outside the main gate and saw his son walking from afar. Just by seeing the way he walked, the father knew immediately that it was his son. "It's my younger son!" he exclaimed. The father ran out and hugged his son. With his eyes, the father didn't see the dirty image of his son, and while the two were embracing one another, the father cried.

The son also cried and said, "Father, I have sinned against heaven and before thee. Now I cannot say that I am your son. I'd just be grateful if you treated me as one of your hired servants."

The father did not listen to what the son was saying but merely said to the servants, "What are you guys doing right now? Hurry up and prepare the bathwater. Bring forth the best robes. You bring my ring and my shoes. The rest of you, kill the fatted calf and let all the neighbors know that my son has returned in good health. Let's have a feast tonight."

The servants' hands then led the son, and they washed his body and hair with warm water. They changed him into nice clothes and cut his hair nice and short. The son's thankfulness could not be expressed in words. When he met his father in his changed image, his father rejoiced, and then his father put a ring upon his hand, which is a symbol of his status as the son, and his father placed shoes upon his feet.

The World of the Heart Changes as It Goes through Six Levels

Literati of the world say that there is no other story like this. According to them, there is no story so short with such deep meanings of life placed within it. This is due to the fact that the structure of the story and the contrasting colors are set very well.

Even if a flower is pretty, if you draw it all in the color red, it is not interesting. In order to express the bright red beauty of a flower well, the flower must stand in contrast to the green leaves and stem. Likewise, there are contrasting colors within the story of the prodigal son, and they are also expressed very well. The prodigal son in the pigpen, rolling around, exhausted and hungry, trying to eat the husks that the swine fed on, is the infinitely dark image. Then there is the image of the son returning to his father's house and putting on the best robes, the ring on his finger, new shoes on his feet, and eating the cooked fatted calf. This is an infinitely bright image.

The story of the prodigal son was not a story of events that actually happened. It was a story that was created. Nevertheless, it has sketched out precisely how the heart of man flows from the beginning to the end. People like the younger son begin by first exalting themselves. Most people do better than others once or twice. They do not remember the wrong they have done very well, but they remember for a very long time the good that they have done. When they make some money or do something that others are unable to do, they feel proud of themselves in their hearts. When they think about those things, they become joyful and proud. As one then two layers of this kind of heart pile up, one on top of another, they harden, leading to the thought "I'm doing well!"

I too have memories of that. When I attended school, I did not have good grades. But when I was in the third grade, there were seventy students in my class. Once, I finished in third place. It was the first time I had ever done that well. When I showed my report card to my father, he was so happy that he took me to my grandfather. "Father, Ock Soo got third place."

My grandpa was very proud of that, and he said, "Wow, that boy!" This was in the third grade. I was ten years old then, so it has been almost sixty years ago, and yet that scene is still vivid in my mind. From then on, I had the heart that I was good at studying.

Also, during a sports meet, there were eight people who ran a race, and I finished first one time. Through that incident, I had the heart "I can run well." This idea took root in my heart. When you have the heart that you are doing well, you become high-hearted. The younger son also had the heart that he was doing well, and with that heart, he became high-hearted. When you become high-hearted, you begin to become negligent and self-indulgent. The younger son took the great wealth received from his father, went to a faraway country, and wasted it all. If your heart is humble, then the prostitute cannot take you, but because the younger son believed in himself, he ended up becoming negligent and self-indulgent. Whoever you are, when you become arrogant, you become riotous. If you live that way, you will surely fail. Even though you do well in business and you make lots of money, if you have the thought "I'm good at business" and have the heart to believe in yourself, then you cannot listen to others. Ultimately, you will be destroyed. Why do people hate being a failure? It's because the heart falls into pain through that.

After having lost everything, the younger son could not eat or sleep properly, and he was unable to wear good clothing.

The next level is when regret begins. People's hearts flow in this manner. Hearts flow in the same way that raindrops fall onto the mountaintops, and then flow to the places that are lower, forming ponds and lakes, and ultimately flow downward to become ocean water. There are also the ways that people's hearts flow as well. People don't become destroyed for no reason. If you think that you are doing well, you become high-hearted. And when you become high-hearted, you cannot listen to what others are saying. You live riotously, following your own thoughts, and then you become ruined. After you are ruined, pain comes to you.

Have you ever seen a person who is in pain because he has failed? Have you ever seen a person who is in pain because he has lost his house and lost his car? Before, this person used to spend money frivolously. Now, he has no food to eat, so he goes to the vegetable market to eat the leftover vegetables that have been thrown away. He cannot buy his children any school supplies. Once you are ruined, these are the kinds of difficulties you go through. Once you go through the difficulty, you regret and then you turn around. The younger son was so hungry after having lost everything; he became regretful and turned around.

"If I keep this up, I'm going to starve to death! In my father's house, even the hired servants have bread enough to spare, and yet I perish with hunger. I should go to my father's house." First of all, if a person returns to his father's house, his life changes, and he becomes happier. This is how all life goes. And that is why success is important, but it is also important to go through failure. You have to also realize you are wrong and sometimes you have to even turn around. There are times when you need to learn from it and turn around. People who have a strong heart to believe in themselves will only surely fail. No matter who you are, you have to know that you can be wrong. You have to be able to see your own blemishes, and you have to be able to feel your wrongfulness.

The story of the prodigal son has precisely sketched out the world of the heart through six levels: The first level is the level of believing in yourself. The second level is the level of negligence and self-indulgence. If a person believes in himself, he becomes negligent. To be completely ruined is the third level. After having lost everything, you are at the fourth level where pain comes upon you. And when you are in pain, then you realize your image and go on to the fifth level. When you realize how foolish it is to believe yourself, then finally, when you enter the sixth level, you receive the blessing.

All people go through these levels. So when you look at a person's heart, you can see very precisely what step that person is at. People who do not have much experience in life are mostly at the first step. It is because they believe in themselves, and they think that they are right. They believe that everything they do will go well so they do not want to listen to other people. On the other hand, if they have done something wrong, even if they have fallen into gambling or drugs or game addiction, if they know the world of the heart precisely, then they can break free from it. That is why no matter who they are, they must learn the world of the heart.

Chapter 2

Desires

Have You Learned Self-Control from a Young Age?

There is no end to a man's desires, but there are limits to a person's ability. Problems arise when our desires exceed our abilities. Chronic complaints about desires ruin life and make everything miserable. That is why training for self-control from a young age is very necessary.

A Leper, Who, for the First Time in His Life, Went to a Chinese Restaurant and Had Jajang Noodles

A long time ago, I once held a conference at the Chungmu leper colony. At that time, we did not have a sedan, so I would take the bus from Daegu to go to Masan, and then I had to take the bus once again from Masan to go to Chungmu. The day of the conference, I got on the bus in Daegu, and there were three strange-looking men sitting on the bus. I looked closely at them, and they were lepers.

I spoke to them first, "Hello. Where are you going?"

"We are going to a church conference," one of them replied.

"Which church conference are you going to?"

"It is the Chungmu Ejo church conference." The three lepers were going to the conference where I was the main speaker. And in order to go there, they had left Ahndong from early in the morning, and we had gotten on the same bus from Daegu.

"Who is the main speaker for that conference?" I asked.

"I heard it is Pastor Ock Soo Park," they replied.

"Have you ever seen Pastor Ock Soo Park?"

"No, not yet!"

"Don't lie."

"No, we haven't."

"I think you are lying."

"No, we've really never seen him." At that time, when I told them that I was Pastor Ock Soo Park, they were so shocked that they almost fainted.

By the time we arrived in Masan, it was already lunchtime. I asked them, "Why don't we eat before we go?" At that time, it was most convenient to go to Chinese restaurants, so I stepped into a Chinese restaurant first, but the three that were following me hesitated to go in. They were hesitant because they were afraid of entering the restaurant, and they were embarrassed because they were lepers. I realized that, and I called them in with an even louder voice. "Hurry up and come in. What are you doing?" The three of them hesitated, but they came in and sat on the chairs. "Excuse me. Four double-sized bowls of jajang noodles," I ordered. The young man who took the order looked at us and knew that there was something strange about the three men, but even so, he silently brought the bowls of jajang noodles. "Hey, young man, bring me some pickled radish and some more onions, please!" That day, we deliciously enjoyed the jajang noodles. Then we once again got on the bus to go to Chungmu, and the three of them appeared to be so happy.

"Pastor, thank you very much! Because of you, I ate jajang noodles for the first time in my life."

Lepers were not allowed to go into restaurants, but they were saying that because of me, they were able to go in. "If I tell my wife about this, she probably won't be able to sleep," one of them said.

One of them also said, "Today is a day that I will never forget for the rest of my life." Back then, I would often meet lepers and preach the Word of God to them. I also spoke with them often. I saw that they lived with so much difficulty because of their leprosy.

Among them, there were many who were very diligent and many who were well educated, yet they had to live a life isolated from society. Once in a while, they would have to go to the city for some business, and they were very careful to not reveal themselves. That is why these lepers were so touched to have a bowl of jajang noodles. The three of them were so excited about eating the jajang noodles that they asked, "Pastor, there are those of us who have never been to the public bathhouse. What does the public bathhouse look like?" And they asked me questions about this and that. They were amazed by anything and overwhelmed by everything. It was because their hearts were low and humble.

A Temp Cleaner and His Son
from a Village in Seoul

When a person lives humbling his heart, a joyful and thankful life is possible. For example, suppose I am a person who is rated at about one hundred, but I think of myself to be two hundred or three hundred. Since there is such a difference in ratings, when conflicts or situations come up, then I will always think that it is because other people are slighting me or despising me. That one thought will cause me to always be dissatisfied with the actions of other people who are dealing with me. On the other hand, if I am a person who is rated at one hundred, but I think of myself to be only thirty or forty, then I will always feel thankful and overwhelmed by the actions of the people around me who are treating me so well.

Once you humble your heart, just as the water flows from a higher place to a lower place, the hearts of the people around you start to flow into you, causing you to always have thoughts of thankfulness. On the other hand, if you become high-hearted, you feel frustrated and full of complaints because of how you judge yourself. Ultimately, the people around you begin to dislike you for being that way. With just the people around you, it may be okay with them because they do not see you every day. However, if you are that way while living with your family, then things will only get worse. If a husband's heart is high, then the wife has to live in misery. If the wife is high-hearted, then the husband has to live in misery, and the children end up living miserably as well. If you become high-hearted, it makes all of the people around you become uncomfortable. Therefore, you must not become high-hearted. However, the nature of a person's heart is to continually become exalted more and more.

Nowadays, gas or oil boilers are mostly used for heating systems, but long ago, charcoal was burnt during the winter for heating. That's why in the past, there would be at least two, three, or even as much as ten trays of ash a day per house. When the charcoal ashes would pile up in front of the doors of each house, the cleaners would come early in the morning, bringing big carts, loading the carts with the charcoal ashes, and hauling them away.

In one village in Seoul, there was a very steep incline, so it was very difficult for the cleaners. At the top of that incline, when there would be snow in the winter, the cleaners would slip and fall. In the village where that steep incline was, there was a cleaner named Cheol Min Kim. Because he was so poor, he lived in a single room with his wife and three children. When he would come home after cleaning the charcoal ashes, he would be so tired that he would have aches and pains the whole night. One day, his eldest son, who was in the sixth grade, heard his father moaning all night and then saw his father wake up early in the morning once again, change clothes, and go back to work.

His wife, who was standing next to him, spoke with a worried heart. "Honey, if you go out with that body of yours and if it gets worse, what are you going to do? If you take one day off, your body will get better. Just take one day off today."

"It is because you don't know what will happen. If I take one day off, then the ashes of the region that I am in charge of would be piled too high. If the district office employee passes by and sees that, because I am not a full-time employee, but just a temp, they will fire me for not working diligently. Then, how are we going to eat, and how are we going to live? I have to get up and go."

If he could have, he would have taken a day off, but the father slowly put on his clothes, put on his gloves, and went outside. It was so heartbreaking for the son to see such an image of his father. The son knew very well the difficulty his father continually had to endure working for the family. That is why, the way this son thought was different from other children. The son of the cleaner would use his notebooks conservatively, not wasting a single page. He would also be very careful with his pencils. And whenever there were things he needed money for in school, he would not ask of his parents and but simply said that he would avoid doing the activities that required money.

One day, while he was studying in school, his father kept coming to his mind. After class, a friend asked, "Hey, let's go over to my house and play." But that son could not do that. He went home and threw his books into the room and immediately ran to the area where his father was working. From afar, he could see his father putting ashes onto the cart and pulling it up the hill. Because it was so heavy and tiring and difficult, the father could not go up straight but rather went up in a zigzag pattern. The son ran and started pushing the cart from behind with all his strength. The father suddenly felt the cart become much lighter. *Who's pushing it?* he thought. But because of the tall pile of ashes, he could not see the person who was pushing. When they reached the crest of the hill and stopped the cart, he looked behind and saw that it was his son. It was his own son, and he felt so thankful to him.

The father then laid the cart to one side and went to the store, bought two large, round moon pies, sat down, and ate them with his son.

"Is it good?" his father asked.

"Yes, it's good. Father, won't you have some more?"

"Did you eat enough?"

"I am fine."

"I am full because I had lunch just a little while ago, but, Father, why don't you have some more?"

"No, I am also full."

"Father, I haven't had this bread treat for a long time. It's so delicious."

The father would think of the son, and the son would think of his father. And although they were poor, the love flowed between their hearts. The son used to feel that it would be embarrassing if his friends at school found out that his father was a cleaner if he were to run into them while pushing his father's cart. However, when the son saw the image of his father who would go out to work for his family despite all his physical pain, he would help his father as soon as he finished school for the day. The father and son, whose hearts were very close, were happy.

The More Abundantly You Live, the Less Time There Is for the Heart to Flow

Nowadays, children rarely have any conversations with their parents. It is because their hearts are so different. When the father sees his son's image, he worries. "What will he grow up to be living like that?" When the father looks at his son and compares him to his generation and his standards of life, his son appears to be so negligent. As a result, the father is full of complaints, and inevitably, even though the father doesn't intend to, he ends up constantly nagging his son. On the other hand, the son, who was filled with complaints to begin with, now complains even more because his father is now nagging. He becomes bitter toward his father and even defies his father. Such things happen because there is no flow of the heart between the parents and their children. If people live only pushing forth their own opinions and following only after their own ambitions, the hearts of the parents and the children will only grow distant.

Regardless of the country, when the economy of a nation develops, the desires of the citizens grow as well. As they begin to have the things that they did not have in the past, their lives become more and more different. So the better off they become, the simple things disappear, and life becomes more complicated. There is now no time for fathers and children or even brothers and sisters to share their hearts. And even when such a time does present itself, everyone is so busy with his or her own things that they all behave so selfishly. Then, once again, there is no time. As they continue to live like this, there is no margin of time for their hearts to flow. In Mr. Cheol Min Kim's family, even though the circumstances of his household and family may have been difficult, the son came to know and understand his father's hardship and became thankful. There are not many families who live like the family of Mr. Cheol Min Kim. It is a special case where, although the family circumstances may be difficult, the son is thankful because he knows the suffering of his father. He goes and helps his father with the work of a cleaner and lives a happy life. On the other hand, while there are families where everyone lives under the same roof, if the hearts do not flow, you cannot call them a true family.

When We Were Poor, We Just Lived through It, but Now, We Earn Lots of Money

There was a person who was a full-time soldier and had nowhere to go after being discharged from the army. A friend of his had an empty room at his family's factory, so he lived in that room with that family for several years. Afterward, however, something happened to that friend, and he had to move out. There was nowhere for him to go immediately, but he found a room to live in, and he worked security at warehouses along the harbor. He received about $1,000 a month, and it was very tight for him to feed his whole family and put his three children through school with only that amount of money.

One day, the son asked his father to buy him some new sneakers. "Dad, my shoes are all worn out."

"Yes, you are right. However, I have already spent my paycheck for this month. You'll have to wait for another month."

"But, Father, the soles are all worn out, and water seeps through."

"I am sorry. Next month, I will surely buy you new shoes when I get paid."

The son understood the circumstances, so he did not press anymore. When it was the day for the next paycheck to arrive, the first thing the father did was take his son to the shoe store. Expensive shoes cost more than a hundred dollars, but he could not afford such shoes for his son. Instead, he bought a no-name brand shoe for only twenty-five dollars. However, the son saw that the heels of his father's shoes were also completely worn out.

"Father, what about your shoes?" the son asked.

"When I go to work, I change immediately into my work boots. So these shoes are just for walking back and forth to work. These worn-out shoes are perfectly fine for that."

"But Father, your shoes are completely worn out. Why don't you get a new pair of shoes too, Father?"

"I can buy them next time. For this month, I am just happy that we can buy your shoes."

The son was very thankful to his father. The father's and the son's hearts became even closer, and it was really great.

"Son, you study hard and become a great man. Don't live like your father, but make good money.

"Yes, Father. But, Father, I still love you."

Time passed by, and one day, the father went to the city to run some errands. While walking on the streets, by chance, he ran into a former senior officer whom he served with in the military.

"Hey, long time no see. How have you been?" asked the former officer.

"Oh, Colonel Kim! How are you?" he replied.

"How long has it been? Why haven't we been in touch?"

"I am sorry. I had been unable to reach you."

"So what are you up to?"

"Oh, I just came into the city to run some errands."

"Really? Then why don't we go get some tea?"

The two of them began to have a conversation as they drank tea together.

"So what line of work are you in these days?"

"Well, I tried hard to find a job, but it didn't go so well, so I work as a security guard at storage warehouses."

"A security guard? When you were in the army, you were so smart, and you were good at what you did."

"No, what was I good at?"

"Listen, I know for a fact that our materials manager is about to quit, and I think his position will be available in about a month or so. Why don't you come and work at our company?"

"Is it okay for a person like me to have that kind of a job?"

"Look, I know you. You'll do fine. I can't pay you much while you are in training. I will pay you \$2,500 a month, and after two months, after you're done with your training, we will pay you \$3,000 a month. It's not much, but it should be enough for you to live without much discomfort. Here is my card. I really hope that you will come and work for me."

"Oh yes. Thank you very much."

He went home in the evening and told his wife what had happened during the day, and his wife was so happy. A few days later, he got a phone call from the company telling him to start the following month. On the first day of work, he put on new shoes he bought with money that he borrowed, put on new clothes, and went to the company.

"Manager, I thought I would be poor my entire life, but I wanted to thank you so much for thinking of a person like me. I will never forget this grace my entire life."

"Look, I know you well, and I know you will do a great job."

"Yes, I will. I will work with all my heart so that I will not cause you any embarrassment, and I will repay you for this, sir."

When he did security work at storage warehouses, he would just sit down all day long, read books, and he wasted his time. But now, he was the manager of supplies, so the work he was doing was a lot of fun. It kept him busy, and the first month passed very quickly. The day he received the $2,500 for his first paycheck, he felt like he had suddenly become very rich. Now at his dining table, foods that he could not afford previously, like expensive mackerel and watermelon, could be served. So he bought some and sat down with his family and ate together. The whole family was happy. A few months passed, and the father's salary went up to $3,500, and their circumstances became even better. As a result, the family was really excited and joyful. But then a problem began to arise. When they had much less, the children didn't expect much. But as the father's earnings increased, their desires started to become greater and greater as well.

One day, the son said to the father, "Father, buy me some sneakers."

"Your sneakers are not worn out yet."

"There's no one in my class who wears the shoes that I wear. They all wear Nike or Puma. Everyone wears those kinds of shoes."

"Before, you said your shoes were fine."

"Father, when we didn't have money, I had no choice, and so I didn't say anything. But now we have money. Since we have enough money, why do we have to continue to appear poor? Please, buy me a pair of Nike shoes. I will wear them when I go to school, and when I come home, I will wear my old shoes."

Now that they had money, the children's desires became greater and greater. When the family was poor, they were thankful for the cheap shoes, and they were able to suppress their heart of wanting to wear expensive shoes. But now, their circumstances had changed. "I want to buy a gift and go to my friend's birthday party." "I want to go out with my friends and buy some hamburgers and have some fun."

The father was shocked. No matter how much money he made, his son's desires grew so much faster than the money that the father made. It became uncontrollable. The father also needed many things. Before, it was not a problem for him to wear worn out shoes, but now that he had to meet many customers, he had to have new shoes and wear a nice, clean suit as well. The way his wife shopped at the markets had also changed. He was surely making much more money. In fact, he was making a considerably large amount of money compared to what he had made before, but it was still not enough. It became uncontrollable because the family's desires had grown larger than the money that he was making. The father and son no longer shared the warm love and attachment they once did. The son began to complain more and more towards his father who could not fulfill all of his desires. In addition, the arguments between the father and son began to grow even more. However, because the father loved his son, although he knew he shouldn't, he still continued to give his son money. His son grew more and more accustomed to spending money, and the words "Give me money" were always hanging on his lips. The relationship between the father and the son only grew sour as time passed.

68

More Important Than a Growing Economy Is the Mind-set to Control One's Self

In 1972, President Jung Hee Park made the Revitalization Federal Law, with the rallying slogan being, "Ten billion dollars in exports and a per capita income of one thousand dollars." At that time, nobody believed that a single person's income could be one thousand dollars. Today, Korea's per capita income exceeds twenty thousand dollars. Compared to then, we live more than twenty times better. In Ulsan, which has a higher per capita income, it is at forty thousand dollars. In Geojae Island, I heard it is thirty thousand dollars. However, are the people of our nation happy? They are not really happy. They have more complaints now, and the rate of people who commit suicide is increasing. It is because as the economy developed, people saw more and wanted more and their desires began to grow at an alarming rate.

A long time ago, mothers lived fine without washing machines, electric rice cookers, refrigerators, or gas ovens. They would carry water pots on their heads, go to the well and draw water, make a fire and use the water to make rice. They would also do the laundry with their hands and they would iron with a flat iron. Even though they lived that way, they were relaxed and they had plenty of time to spare and time to speak to their children. When I look at my wife today, she has so many convenient machines that she cannot be compared with my mother. Even so, I don't know why she's so busy. The way in which my wife and I raised our children, versus how my son and his wife raise our grandchildren is also quite different. We raised our children in such a way that they would understand the importance of conserving, but my son and his wife raise their children in the midst of abundance. Even so, my daughter-in-law is busier than my wife.

As life became more abundant through economic advancement, desires have grown faster than anything else. When the per capita income grows from ten thousand to twenty thousand dollars, desires reach the levels of thirty and forty thousand dollars. It is difficult for the economy to grow at a high-speed rate, but desires can grow overnight. Even as people live in a time when most people earn twenty thousand dollars, if their desires remain at ten thousand dollars, then they can be happy buying clothes, a car, and enjoying any kind of food. They would then be happy no matter what they did. However, if they live in a time where they make twenty thousand dollars, but their desires are at forty thousand dollars, then their abilities cannot keep up with their desires. As a result, they cannot spend their money according to their desires. Therefore, they are full of complaints when they buy a car, full of complaints when they buy clothes, full of complaints when they eat food, and full of complaints no matter what they do. That is why, although we do need economic growth, more importantly, we need to have the mind-set to practice self-control.

Parents Need to Hold Back the Heart of Wanting to Do Things for Their Children, and the Children Need to Break Their Hearts of Asking for Things

I learned the world of the heart through the Bible. I have a son and a daughter, and for my children to live happily, I felt that I needed to instill within them the heart to control their desires within them. When my children were young, they were satisfied with candy or ice cream. However, even though they turn twenty, if they continue to say, "Daddy, candy. Daddy, ice cream," they are fools. In reality, as children grow older, their desires become greater and they expect more things: "Dad, buy me a bicycle. Dad, buy me a computer. Dad, buy me a cell phone." Their desires also become bigger at higher speeds. In the same way, there are not many fathers who are able to accede to all of their children's growing desires. No matter how rich a person may be, because the desires of children grow at such a high speed, there will come a certain point where the father's ability is unable to keep up with the growing desires. At that moment, when the father is unable to fulfill those desires, the children begin to live with complaints and bitterness in their hearts.

When my son pressed me to buy him something, even though I did have the ability to buy everything for him, I would purposely not allow him to have a few things. Actually, when a father takes his son's hand and buys him what he wants, and he sees his child rejoicing, that makes the father really happy. On the other hand, when the father does not have money and is unable to buy his child what he wants, then the father is very tormented. That is the innate heart of parents. Therefore, if the father misjudges, he may think that it is right to simply give in to every desire of his son. The son will then ultimately become a problematic child. That is because he will despise his father who is unable to supply him with all his desires.

When you try to learn a new language past the age of fifty, it is very difficult. A foreign language is easier to learn, the younger you are. My grandchildren who live in America speak English well. When I speak English, the kids laugh. They mean that my pronunciation is wrong. When a person who has spoken Korean for a long time speaks English, the pronunciation does not come out precisely. You have to learn from a young age in order to have the correct pronunciation. If you learn how to speak English in your twenties, you may able to speak well, but your pronunciation will not be precise. That is why it is better to learn a language from a very young age. Even the ability to control your desires must also be learned from your youth. When a child gets older and tries to learn this, then it requires much more effort, and it becomes extremely difficult. When I was raising my children, I purposely did not give in to their desires, and instead, I "broke" their desires. Even though my children would pressure me by crying, "Daddy," I did not give in to them. Once, when my son was in middle school, he asked me for some money.

"Father, there is a Tae Kwon Do exam to get the first degree, and I need fifty dollars to pay for the judging fee."

"Why do you have to pay fifty dollars to be judged?"

"It's not from our studio, but this is the World Tae Kwon Do Headquarters that is running it. That's why I have to pay for the judging fee."

"Hey, if you pay the fifty dollars, are you sure that you can get your first degree black belt?"

"Yes, I know I can pass."

"How?"

"It's because it is a studio that only allows people who have already passed the first round to take the test. That's why I know I can get my first degree."

"Good. Then, you are already a first degree. It's just that the association has not recognized it. Now, you can quit Tae Kwon Do."

He wanted to get his first degree and he felt wronged to have to quit. But what can he do? My son broke his heart and quit Tae Kwon Do. When my son was studying in high school and college he occasionally told me,

> Thank you, Father. Father, I truly thank you for raising me the way you did. The kids at my school are unable

to control themselves, and it is very saddening to see them going through so much, just because they are unable to control themselves. Father, if you had not broken my heart, I too would have been that way. I would've just lived doing whatever I wanted.

At first, when he heard that his friends in class would go skiing on the weekends, he felt so envious of them. On Sundays, my son had to drive the church shuttle and work all day long at the church. He couldn't go skiing. Most students depart on Saturday to go skiing and return home on Sunday afternoon. The next time, they would go skiing until Monday and come to school on Tuesday. Later on, they would come to school on a Wednesday. In America, no one reprimands students for this kind of behavior. If the teacher demands that the students study, the belief is that such a request would be infringing on the students' personal rights. Instead, they can only say that studying is good. In this way, children who have not received the training to control their minds, get their hands on drugs and occasionally, they are unable to graduate from school. As my son saw this, his heart was thankful towards me. He said that because I did not listen to all his desires and disciplined his heart, he was able to not step out of line.

Even Now, You Need to Learn to Break Your Desires and Humble Your Heart

More than anything else, it is more important for children to learn to break their hearts from an early age. Even if the parents are great teachers, famous politicians, or great businessmen, if they do not know the world of the heart, they just want to be unconditionally good and give their children everything. As they give in to everything that their children want, they want to rear their children to be great people. Rare are the parents who teach them to control their hearts and to refrain from their desires. If there are young people who have not yet learned how to control their desires and how to discipline their hearts, although it may be late, even now they must learn how to discipline their hearts. It is easier to do it now than it would be when you become older. If you try to break children's hearts in their adolescent age rather than doing it while they are young, you will find that your children will rebel. And when they feel that the relationship isn't going to work out, they end up running away from home. When they are about five or six years old, they are unable to run away from home so they are forced to break their hearts. But as they get older, instead of breaking their hearts, they look for ways to get around it.

Many people who are serving their sentences in prison today are people who could not break their desires well. They simply had to do whatever it was they wanted to do, and they did not hesitate. Ultimately, they entered into a life of crime. In this world, there is no one who can do whatever he or she wants. Be it a government minister or a president, we cannot simply do whatever we want. In the newspapers, we often see people who could not control their desires. And even though they may be in high positions, they fall mercilessly in a single moment. However, people who have "broken" themselves from an early age, even though they have grown older, when they want to do something negative, they are able to think, "This is something I should not do. I need to refrain from doing this." They say this and they draw a clear line in their hearts. However, there are people who are completely unable to do this. When they want to do something and the conditions do not allow them to do it, that person has no power to refrain from trying to satisfy their desires. They simply end up becoming criminals.

No matter who it is, if a person becomes high-hearted, that person later becomes pitiful. Because people don't know about the world of the heart, when they become well off circumstantially, they become high-hearted. And when they get good results from doing something well, they also exalt their own hearts. Just like I mentioned in the previous chapter, the younger son thought himself to be so great and did not listen to anyone else's advice. He simply did whatever he wanted to and lived according to his own desires. Such a person can only suffer through difficulty and pain, and will only run into misery. We must learn how not to exalt our hearts, but to humble our hearts instead. We must learn how to control our desires. Then, we can become truly happy.

Chapter 3

Self-Control

Your Ability to Control Yourself Is the Safety Device to Freely Utilize Your Youth

When you can fully trust the function of the brakes, then a car is able to travel at maximum speed. In order to do the things you want as much as you'd like, you must nurture your ability for self-control. In other words, you must hold back from what you want and do the things you don't want. That kind of training to discipline the heart is absolutely necessary. Your ability for self-control is the safety device that allows you to optimally maximize your youth.

People Who Continue to
Live, Even though They Know
Their Disease of the Heart

When I see the visually impaired, I think about how uncomfortable their lives must be. They cannot see the faces of their families, and they cannot know exactly what the blue sky and mountains look like. How uncomfortable is it for a healthy person to injure his leg and have to lie there, not being able to do anything? He would be counting the days looking toward a quick recovery. This is also true when your liver or heart is unhealthy. You ask yourself, "Why do I feel so tired? Why am I so fatigued?" and then you get yourself examined at the hospital. When you discover something is wrong, you put all other things aside and address the disease first. Even if you had to spend all the money you have, you'd look for the most reputable doctor, and even want to receive surgery.

People are compelled to heal their sicknesses and diseases when they have ailments in their bodies. However, people are very insensitive about becoming diseased and having diseases of the heart. This is because there is no one who speaks to them precisely about the diseases of the heart. As a result, even though they have diseases in their hearts, they just go on living. People who think that they are great continue to live in arrogance, causing wrinkles and frowns on the foreheads and faces of the people around them. However, because they don't know the world of the heart, they continue living in and enjoying the perception of their own greatness.

There are other people who are always falling into a feeling of insecurity. They don't know how to repair themselves from that state. All they know is, "I feel so insecure in my heart," and they don't know how to cause this insecurity to depart from them. As a result, they continue living in insecurity. There are those who always pick on other people's flaws, those who always change their minds, and those who close their hearts to others and just live inside their own worlds.

As I read the Bible, I felt, *Ah, this is how our hearts were formed*, and I came to know the world of the heart. When I applied the world of the heart to my own heart, strangely, my life began to change so much that I couldn't recognize it any longer. Afterwards, whenever I met young college students, I spoke to them about the world of the heart. They listened to me with much curiosity and sincerity.

The Cause of Living Riotously According to Your Own Heart

Along time ago, as an education committee member at the Suwon and Dajeon prisons, I counseled and taught the Bible to prisoners for quite a while. When I first went to the prisons, I was amazed, thinking, "I read about that person in the newspaper, but here he is." In the prisons, I was able to see all the famous people who were featured in newspapers for their crimes.

When I went to the Suwon prison, there was a person named, Jae Sun Yoo, who was in charge of gathering the prisoners and assisting me. He was one of the best-behaved prisoners in the prison, and he acted as the prison captain. When I would meet and speak with him, he was such a kind and pure-hearted person that you couldn't expect anything else to come out of him. I became closer and closer to him, and as time passed, I grew curious. "What crime did he commit that he ended up in here? Did a nice guy like him steal something? I don't think so. Did he commit fraud?" I started to think this to myself. It is considered rude to ask prisoners in prison about the crimes they have committed, but my heart of curiosity grew bigger and bigger inside me. One day, the two of us were just sitting down and talking with one another. I finally asked him what crime he had committed. He had been talking very excitedly, but at that moment his face turned red and he answered, "Murder and attempted murder." I was shocked. "What? You killed someone, and tried to kill some-one else?" I could not believe it. In my eyes, it seemed that he couldn't kill a fly, so I couldn't comprehend how he was able to kill another human being. Afterwards, he told me how he ended up killing someone, and how he got arrested while attempting murder.

This person lived in Busan, got married, had a son, and was forming a happy family. Even though he didn't make much money from his job, it was enough for him and his family to live on without any shortcomings. One day, however, he could tell there was something strange about his wife. She was hiding something from him. He became suspicious, and after one or two months, found out that his wife was going out dancing without his knowledge.

You should dance at home. I don't know why you have to go out to dance. In my experience, people in Africa dance very naturally in their daily lives; therefore, people do not consider it a bad thing to go dancing. When I went to a conference in Nairobi, Kenya, one choir said that they would come and perform for me. We asked to borrow the hall at the hotel, and we prepared coffee and tea. The choir came; they sat us down, and sang to us. Korean people sing with tension in their faces, but the Africans were singing so freely. The entire choir was dancing and singing together. These unique songs pulled out all the emotions from within. All of a sudden, the leader of the choir told me to come out to the front. He wanted us to dance together. I am unlearned in many things, but I am even more than unlearned when it comes to dancing. However, if I argued about not going up to the front, I thought I would ruin the atmosphere, so I just went up and tried hard to mimic the people around me.

But in our country, dancing is considered something bad. When he thought that his wife was going out dancing, he felt as though the sky was crumbling down. He threatened his wife, he begged her, and even earnestly pleaded, "Please, stop going dancing. Please, stop going out." However, he could not control her. He found out that it was his older sister-in-law who enjoyed dancing, and she was taking his wife with her. When you get married, you get married because of your wife. Nobody gets married because of the sister-in-law, correct?

One day, this man went to his sister-in-law. "Please, I beg you. Stop taking my wife out dancing," he sincerely requested. The sister-in-law replied, "Who do you think you are? You took my little sister, and all you have done for her is made her suffer. How dare you tell me what to do?"

She then poured degrading words all over him. At that moment, this man he just snapped and flipped out. After a while, when he had returned to his senses, there was a knife in his hand and his sister-in-law was lying dead in front of him. With the knife in his hand, he said, "I am going to kill everybody in this family," and continued the chaos. "It's all over now. You will die and I will die," he said.

As he explained the situation, he was telling me, "Even now, I can't really believe that I killed my sister-in-law." Surely, the knife was in his hand and the blood was on his knife, and he saw that his sister-in-law was dead. In that short moment, when he had lost his mind, that's what had happened. He received his judgment and was sentenced to die. Even though his family hired a lawyer for him, he refused. "I am going to die. That's the end of it. I don't need anything, so get out." The third time the lawyer came to him, the lawyer said one thing, "Mr. Yoo snap out of it. Do you think I came here to make money? The money I get from defending you can't even buy me one drink. I came here because I felt sorry for your life, and this is your attitude? If you don't want it, forget it." The lawyer then calmed down and spoke to him again saying, "Mr. Yoo, come here and sit down." While he listened to the lawyer, he felt he was right. He went to court and was serving his sentence.

He thought, "I am going to become a well-behaved prisoner and quickly get out of here to get my revenge. I will have my vengeance on those who have destroyed my life." With that heart, he became a well-behaved prisoner. He eventually changed his heart, and threw away his hatred and vengeance. He has since been released and has formed a new family and is now living a happy life.

Even now, I vividly remember everything. He said that he could feel that there was something, outside of him, which was leading him to the edge, to darkness, and to destruction. There was this invisible tragic force he could feel that was leading his family, his children, and everything else to destruction. Through that story, I was able to know, "Prison is not a place where some special people go. This is how people end up after committing sin." After counseling the prisoners for about one year, I came to know precisely why people end up in prison. Of course, this is not true in every case, but prisoners, for the most part, are people who have not lived disciplining their desires from a young age. They were dragged according to the thoughts that arose in their hearts to do the things that they wanted to do. Even though they lived diligently, in one instant instance, they were unable to control their hearts when it came to women, money, or honor. And often times, the tower they had spent their entire lives building would collapse overnight.

It Is the Brakes that Must Overcome the Engine

A few years ago, three thousand college students from all over the world gathered in Korea for the IYF World Camp. At that time, I told them, "Hyundai Motors can produce a car every thirteen seconds (It's now every five seconds)." One of our African students was completely shocked and said, "Pastor, how can you make a car every thirteen seconds? That makes no sense." "I don't know how, but that's what the statistics say." "But Pastor, how can a car be made in thirteen seconds?"

Because of this, I had the students from the World Camp visit the Hyundai Motors factory. When I told Hyundai Motors that there would be three thousand students visiting, they were shocked and said, "Please, bring just one thousand per day." So, we divided them into three groups and visited the Ulsan factory. I followed along on the first floor of the factory where they were working on the assembly line. Up towards the ceilings, they made walkways with safety bars for us to tour the factory. From up there, we could see the entire process of how a car was made. There was a conveyor belt installed on the assembly floor and the car frame was placed on it. The frame would then be carried slowly along on the conveyor belt where the technicians would work on the parts that they were in charge of.

The first technician lays the electrical lines throughout the chassis. From the moment he starts until he gets off work, all he does is lay out electrical lines. The next technician places a cover on top of it. The conveyor belt moves on, and they install the seats into the car. It is a robot that does this. It is not easy to fit seats into a small chassis, but the robots put the seats in specific positions. They then begin to drill, the seats are bolted in and the installation is quickly completed. Soon afterwards, they install the engine. Towards the end of the assembly line is the robot that performs all of the welding. This is how 30,000 parts come together to make a car. At the very end, the cars are fueled, driven out of the factory and parked in a large outdoor parking lot.

I actually witnessed a car being completed in approximately one minute. If there are five conveyor belts such as this one, then it is true that a car is being made every twelve seconds. When the students who could not believe that a car was made every thirteen seconds visited the factory, they simply nodded their heads. At the Hyundai Motor factory, they always do road tests on fully assembled cars. The most important part of a car is the engine. The power created from the engine is delivered to the wheels to make the car move forward. The next most important things are the brakes, which bring the car to a stop. And the most efficient brake system will actually bring the car to a stop even when the weather conditions make it seem impossible.

Nowadays, even when driving on sheets of ice, a car does not slip when ABS brakes are used. However, when I was young, cars did not have the best braking systems. Back then, there would be a wire that would pull on the brakes so, when you stepped on the brakes it was similar to stepping on the brakes when riding a bicycle. Therefore, even though you stepped on the brakes, the car would often slip. If you were in a truck going downhill that had a lot of cargo, no matter how much you stepped on the brakes, the truck would continue to slip. Therefore, oftentimes, the driver would have to literally stand up and pull on the steering wheel as he stepped down hard on the brakes.

While the engine is the part of the car that causes the car to go fast, the car is able to go fast because it has brakes. With brakes, even though the car is traveling at its highest speed, it can come to a stop when there are objects in front of it. On the other hand, without brakes, the car cannot come to a sudden stop. Even though the engine may be strong, if the brakes don't work properly, the car can't be driven. It is now a dangerous machine. Of course, good cars need to be able to travel fast, but they also need to be able to stop when they have to. It is for this reason that the technicians pair the engine against the brakes during the final road tests. When they step on the accelerator as much as possible, and then apply the brakes, should the car stop or continue moving? It should stop. The brakes must defeat the engine. Then, it is a safe car.

The Engine and Brakes of Man's Heart Are Desire and Self-Control

The world of a person's heart is exactly like a car. Just as the car has an engine, in a person's heart there is the desire to strive to do something. When we see food, we have the desire to eat the food. "That apple looks delicious. That ice cream looks good." People who suffer because of money, work hard to make money, and study to figure out how they can make lots of it. There are also people who yearn to be famous in the future. "I want to become a broadcast announcer. I want to become a baseball player." In that way, the desires of our bodies and hearts lead us to certain actions. If young people become lost without any desires at all, then they become good for nothing in life. It is only natural for young people to be filled with curiosity, and it is only natural for them to have many things they want to do.

Long ago, when I would go for walks with my son, I would walk straight ahead, but my son would jump around and go into the neighbor's yard to pluck the leaves off the persimmon trees. He would also kick cans that were in front of him. Because I was older, I was unable to do those things, but because my son was so full of energy, he couldn't just walk straight. Young people are overflowing with energy, so they want to "do things." They even have dreams that are not easy to accomplish. "I want to become a great doctor in the future. I want to become a great politician. I want to become a great pianist. I want to become a great soccer player." Because these desires arise in them, even though they want to play, they suppress the desire, and instead, they study hard and practice. Desire is like the engine of a car. In the same way that an engine causes a car to move forward, there is an energy that leads people to move forward. It causes people to concentrate while studying, and allows them to withstand challenges so that they can continue to work hard.

But there's something important here. A person should not only have desires, but he or she needs brakes to slow them down. People should not just continue to move forward simply because they want to; but they should also know how to slow down and even stop. Sometimes, we want to have fun or play computer games. Then we come to a point when we say to ourselves, "I've played the game too long. Now I need to study. These games are preventing me from studying." You should be able to step on the brakes in this way. You absolutely need the "brakes of the heart" to stop what you are doing and do something else. If you only have desires and no strength to control them, it is like driving a car without brakes. It is too dangerous. When your abilities, the times, or the circumstances do not allow you to do certain things, and you don't have the strength to control your self, you become miserable. When you build a house, first you design the house and lay the foundation according to those designs. You install the pillars, set up the walls, and then you lay down the roof. In this way, a house can be completed in the proper order. On the other hand, if you thoughtlessly begin with the roof, how difficult would that be? Life is exactly the same. If we think, we can say to ourselves, "I have to work hard to get these things under control." Then we can make plans. However, if we plan without thinking, and only follow our desires, we will fall into hardship.

What Kinds of People
Fall Into Drugs?

The situation in every country is different, but I once heard that drugs are easily accessible in America. In Korea, drugs are hard to come by, so most students have nothing to do with drugs. However, in environments where drugs are easily placed in their hands, students become largely divided into two groups. There are students who are opposed to taking drugs and students who take drugs and become addicted. Do you know what kind of students are the ones who become drug addicts? They are the ones who overly believe in themselves. One friend says, "This is nothing. Just because you do this once, it's not going to be that bad. It's okay," and slowly pressures his friend. At that moment, a student who does not believe in himself will see the drugs and say, "If I touch that, I am going to ruin my life like the guy across the street. That guy lives his whole life in darkness because of drugs. I heard that once you fall into drugs, you can never escape them." Then the student will become afraid and avoid it. However, the student who trusts himself will say, "Okay. Just doing it once won't make me addicted. I will just try once and that will be it." And with curiosity, he accepts the drugs.

However, when someone does drugs once, the heart of wanting to do it again is greater than before: "Doing it twice is not going to affect me. I'll just do it a second time and then I'll stop." But after doing it a second time, the heart of wanting to do it again becomes even greater: "What? Just because I did it three times…" Following this pattern, they do it three times, four times, and later on, they will say, "Forget it," and just throw themselves away altogether. People who believe in themselves fall into the drugs little by little, and ultimately become drug addicts for the rest of their lives. They eventually end up living in pain and misery. People who believe in themselves do not use discretion. They just think that nothing is a big deal. They consider everything to be insignificant, and if there's a problem, they think, "I will just take care of it then." This is what they think. Most people with that heart wind up in prison or addicted to drugs.

The Couple Who Could only Become Divorced because Both of Them Thought that They Were Great

Once, I was counseling a young woman who had previously been married. The young woman told me that she had gotten divorced two and a half years ago. I asked her why she got divorced, and she said it was because she did not like her husband's personality. When I hear such things I cannot help but laugh. If the personalities don't fit, then all you have to do is make them fit. All you have to do is discuss this with your husband and say, "My personality is like this and your personality is like that, so why don't we work this out?" But if you don't know the world of the heart, you don't want to break your heart and accept the words of your husband. You just want your husband to break his heart to meet your needs. The husband, on his end as well, wants his wife to fit him. Since high-hearted people only exalt their own perspectives in this way, people's hearts cannot fit with one another. So, I asked her once again, "Do you have an air conditioner at home?"

"Yes."

"When you install an air conditioner, and it starts to get cool in the beginning, later on, when the cold air is very strong and it causes you to shiver, do you remove the air conditioner and throw it away?"

"No. I simply adjust it with the remote control." she replied.

"Suppose you bought a new TV and it was so loud that it blew the whole neighborhood away. Would you throw that TV away?"

"No, I would adjust the volume."

I have seen many machines until now, but I've never seen a machine made as well as a human. What machine is there that is as sophisticated as a human being? No matter how you program or set a boiler, can it always be exactly 98.6°F in the building? It is impossible. Where is the boiler inside of a human body? Is it in the stomach? Is it in the chest, or in the heart? We have no boiler in our bodies, yet we always maintain the same temperature. Boilers use different kinds of fuels like wood, charcoal, kerosene, or gasoline. For example, you cannot use gasoline in a kerosene boiler. However, people can maintain body heat even though they eat ice cream. They can maintain their body heat whether they are eating cabbage or eating rice. I have no idea how we could be this perfectly made. When we take a look at this, we can see that man is so sophisticated that man cannot be compared to an air conditioner or a television.

So I said to her, "We could never compare something as inexpensive as an air conditioner or a television to a human being. But even the cheap air conditioners and televisions have the ability to be adjusted. Then wouldn't humans also have the ability to adjust?" The woman just continued to stare blankly at me. I told her, "You may not know it, but it's there." Because people do not know that their hearts have the ability to adjust, people who have no reason to be divorced get divorced. The people who have no reason to fight, fight. And the people who have no reason to go to prison, end up in prison. "Has your husband remarried?" I asked. "No, he has not," she replied.

I then met her husband later. Compared to his wife, he was a very capable person. He was an upright person who was well known in the community and extremely smart. I told him to reconcile with his wife. I could see that he was very lonely after the divorce, and when I told him to reconcile with his wife, he welcomed the idea. Their children were the happiest about this, and the parents on both sides of the family were also very happy as well. These two people who had lived in unspeakable pain after their divorce now live so happily together.

One day, that husband came to see me and said, "Pastor, do you know why my wife and I got divorced?"

"I heard that it was because you didn't get along with one another."

"No, that's not why.'"

"That was what your wife told me."

"That's not true."

"Then why did you get divorced?"

"We were people whose futures could only lead to divorce. I thought that because I was so great that I could live without her. But the bigger problem was that my wife was five times greater than I was. Because we both thought we were so great, we only wanted to follow our own opinions. That's why our marriage could only end in divorce."

People Today Who Live Having Lost the Ability to Contemplate

When people don't have the ability to control themselves, they try to live according to their own will. Then after they make a few mistakes, they begin to think about how wrong they were. "Why did I yell that time? Why was I so narrow-minded? How did I make that decision without seriously thinking it through?" There are many people who have such regrets. But if we live our lives however we want, only pain and regret will remain. We have to first think deeply and nurture the ability to control our desires. Nowadays, everyone is so busy that there is no time or room to think deeply about anything. And through the advancement of the entertainment business, TV, and computer games, people only reach the first level of thought. They are unable to get to the second level of thought.

A long time ago, the people of China and Korea enjoyed playing Chinese chess. There was competition between the Han Dynasty and the Chu Dynasty. In this game, there is the king, the advisor that protects the king, the chariot, the cannon, the horse, the elephant, and the regular soldiers. These two nations battle on the chessboard, and as they play, the two players must think deeply. When the enemy's elephant comes forward, we you must start to think, "Why did it come forward? It's going to get killed by the chariot. Ah, he has a 'canon' behind this piece waiting to strike." This is how players think as they play the game, move by move. They try one strategy, and then they try a different one.

When each player thinks deeply about what his or her opponent will do, then there is the mental or psychological fight. It even comes to the point where others watch thinking, "Where are the two chess players? Why are the chess pieces not moving?" If you mindlessly play chess according to how things appear in your eyes, then you will quickly fall victim to the trap that the enemy has set up for you. You must first observe the plan of the enemy and then act accordingly.

Julio, the drug addict that I spoke about in the first chapter, did drugs for twenty years, but he did not think deeply at all. Without any thought, whenever he would get money, he would do drugs. While living like this, he ate a spoiled piece of bread one day and fell into a thought, "How did I ever become a drug addict? Why do I live like this, unable to eat food that is good? I just live as a lonely man without ever owning my own car or house." If he had just a few dollars, he could buy and eat warm food. Since he spent all his money on drugs, he found himself picking out the spoiled bread from the trash. For the first time in his life, he began to realize just how pathetic he was. "If I become ill, then who will take me to the hospital? If I die, who will mourn for me?" Thinking about the situation that he was in is what helped him to truly understand how pitiful he really was. Had Julio not thought deeply about this, he would have lived the rest of his life as a drug addict, and that is how his life would have ended.

After thinking deeply, a completely different heart entered him. That heart changed his life. When he re-entered rehab, it was only then that the words of the counselor began to enter his heart. He followed the words of the counselor and was able to break free from drugs.

We need to monitor our children's recreational activities as well. While it is important to allow young children to play hard outside, we must also have them develop the ability to reason through games that make them think. In Tetris, if you place the falling pieces in the correct angles and empty slots, then those perfectly filled lines disappear. That's the kind of the game it is. At first, the shapes are coming down slowly, so it is easy to fit them into the spaces without any gaps or empty slots. Later on, though, they pour down like rain, and you have no time or space to think at all. Your hands have to move according to your instincts. These days you cannot think deeply to play games. You have to just react quickly with your senses. But when you play such games for a long time, it deteriorates your ability to reason.

It is along these lines that TV has been called the "idiot box." If I say this, some people may say, "How can you say such a thing? Do you know how much we can learn from TV?" It is true that you can get a wide variety of information and knowledge through television, but it keeps us from being able to think deeply. Think about it. When you are reading a difficult book and you don't understand its meaning, you have to read it two or three times in order to understand it. But with television, even though you change the channel abruptly, if you watch for only five minutes, you can understand the storyline. You don't have to think about it deeply. You can understand it even while you eat. Even though you wake up in the middle of sleeping, half awake, as you watch the television while rubbing your eyes, you can still understand everything. There is no one who strains the brain trying to understand television. So when you watch television often, it may be fun, but because you are only dealing with things that are easily understood, it continually weakens your ability to reason. Later on, you end up turning into a person who cannot think. When you cannot think, whenever you face things in life, you just run into it thoughtlessly without detailed preparation. You just try it and see what happens. People like this often end up falling onto the wrong path.

The Mother Who Buried a Large Piece of Gold in the Ground

In China, there lived a mother and her son. Because they were very poor, the son would gather wood from the mountains and take it to the market and sell it. That was how they were able to eat and barely live every day. When there was rain or snow and the son could not go up to the mountains to get wood, then that day, he would have to go hungry. Therefore, the son always made sure that he went to the mountain every day. Although they were poor, he was an extremely good son to his mother.

When the son was of age to get married, the mother did not have any money and was unable to send him off to marry. This caused her much worry and it broke her heart. "I don't know about anything else, but I wish I could have a daughter-in-law. All I need is just a little bit of money," she thought. That day, the son went to gather wood, and the mother was sweeping the yard with a broom. But, starting from a long time ago, there was always this one big rock in the yard that she would trip over. She tried to remove it, but she couldn't. One day she tried to remove it by digging around the rock with a hoe. After looking at it awhile, she saw that it was not a normal color. She then wondered what it was and decided to pour some water over it and wash it. It was actually a large piece of gold. The moment she saw this, her heart started pounding like a person who had been caught stealing. She quickly buried it. "Ah, I can't believe that we have such a big piece of gold in our own yard," she thought. From that day on, the mother could not sleep. When she would lie down at night she thought about all the things she could do with that piece of gold. "If I break up that piece of gold and sell just a small portion of it, then I could buy a house and afford to send my son off to marriage." While thinking about those things, she could not sleep for several days. Eventually, the mother's face did not look well, and so her son became worried.

"Mother, are you ill?" he asked.

"No, no. I'm okay."

"But you haven't even eaten much."

"No, I'm okay."

As usual, the son would go to the mountain to get wood, and the mother, would sit in the room and would once again, fall into her thoughts. Just imagining the things she could do with that piece of gold overwhelmed her heart. The mother thought about it even further. "If my son realizes that we have a piece of gold in our home, then would my son continue to go to the mountains to gather wood? He wouldn't go. Then what would he do?" The mother had heard that the children from rich families in the village below the mountain would usually go to the bars, hang out and gamble. That's how they lived. Although her son was diligent for the time being, it seemed to her that if he found out about the piece of gold, he would not gather wood anymore. Instead, he would hang out with the rich children, drinking and gambling.

"If my son gambles and loses everything, he's going to need money. Then he's going to come and ask me for another piece of gold. But if I start to hate him for gambling and I do not give him any gold, then he and I will end up getting into a fight." When she quietly thought about it, it seemed that her son would no longer obey her. If that were the case, it seemed to her that they would not be happy even if they became rich.

Then the mother thought about it even further for several days and came to a conclusion. "With that piece of gold, we may be able to live in a big house, eat expensive food, and wear good clothes, but the relationship between my son and I will become crippled. Ultimately, it will be like we were strangers." So then one day, the mother said to her son,

"Son, there's something I want to tell you."

"Say anything you would like, Mother."

"These days, every night I have dreams about dying. It seems that if I continue living in this house, I don't think I can live much longer. I've lived my life to the fullest, so it's okay if I die. But when I think about you being left alone, it breaks my heart. So I think I am going to have to live longer. I hope that we can move somewhere else."

"Mother, what's so hard about that?"

"Do you think that's possible? Okay. Thanks."

Not long after, the mother and son moved to a place that was very far away. They could no longer find their way back, and they continued living in their new home, gathering wood. The piece of gold simply remained at that house, buried.

When people hear these stories, they will say, "How foolish! All they had to do was take that piece of gold and work hard. Why did they leave the gold behind and move away?" People who are unable to adjust their mindsets think this way. When people who without disciplined hearts have many possessions, they stand a great chance of bringing tribulations upon themselves rather than happiness. However, if you do not have desire in your heart, it means you are not human. No matter who you are, everyone wants to eat well and be well educated. Everyone wants to have nice things and marry a great woman. Everyone has such desires. However, if you have only those desires, then that is incomplete. You need to have self-control that is stronger than your desires. This is so you can actually put the brakes on those desires. In America, a lot of lottery winners who became multi-millionaires overnight ended up unhappier than before. Why? Because the ability to put the brakes on the new desires that come with having more money than you are used to having, is weaker than the desire. Then once again, desire suffocates self-control.

You must Nurture Your Ability to Contemplate and Your Ability of Self-Control

We must live thinking about things deeply. We must think deeply and become free from the foolishness of trusting ourselves. The engine of a car is important, but the vehicle itself must absolutely have brakes. In the same way, you must refrain from the things you want to do, and do things that you don't want to do so that from a young age, you are trained to rule and discipline your heart. If you learn how to think deeply and control yourself from a young age, no matter what you do, you can become a great person in that field. If you do not have the ability to control yourself, you can only become miserable. Just as the functions of the engine and the brakes must reach a high level of performance in order for the car to run well, it is the same with our lives. There are many things young people want in their hearts. We do have the ability to run towards those things. Studying hard, researching, and practicing. The images of these things look so good. But what you must remember is that you must nurture your ability to restrain yourself at the same time.

Chapter 4

Wisdom

True Wisdom Is Knowing Your Shortcomings

People think that they are good. They may not express it outwardly, but inside they believe, "I'm better than others in this." That is due to the insularity of never having met someone greater than themselves.

Doctor, Four-Fourths of Your Life Is Sinking into the River

From time to time in life, people are deceived. When this happens, they are unable to believe in others. So instead of believing in others, they end up believing only in themselves. People who believe only in themselves accept whatever they think exactly as it is. Living like this is extremely insecure and dangerous. And because no one is perfect, no matter who it may be, a person's judgment cannot *always* be right. This is why, after he makes a decision, he needs to follow up to see whether or not his judgment was right or wrong. But people who believe in themselves live following their own thoughts without going through the process of examining themselves.

There was an elderly boatman who made money by ferrying people across a river in his small boat. Because there weren't many customers, he would cross the river only three or four times a day. One day, a successful doctor who was originally from that town wanted to cross the river. The boatman began to row his boat. This doctor had left his hometown at a young age, studied hard, and became a famous man. When he looked closely at the boatman, he realized that it was the same boatman who had been rowing the boat when he first left the village. In the doctor's eyes, this man, who had spent his entire life as a boatman, seemed so pathetic. So in an effort to show off the fact that he was well educated, the doctor began to speak to the boatman.

"Mr. Boatman."

"Yes, Doctor?"

"Mr. Boatman, do you know anything about philosophy?"

"What is philosophy? I've never heard of that in my entire life."

"You don't know anything about philosophy? Life itself is a philosophy. If you are living without knowing what philosophy means, it means that one-fourth of your life is as good as dead."

The boatman was a bit offended after listening to the doctor, but because he didn't have a formal education, he couldn't really say anything. He remained silent. Soon afterward, the doctor asked him another question.

"Mr. Boatman."

"Yes, Doctor?"

"Mr. Boatman, do you know anything about literature?"

"Literature? What is that? I know *liter*, and I know *ature*, but I don't know what literature is."

"How in the world is that possible? Mr. Boatman, if you had known what literature is, you could have written such beautiful literature yourself while you lived on this beautiful riverside. You are telling me that you don't know any literature? Mr. Boatman, two-fourths of your life is as good as dead."

Because these were words that were coming from a famous doctor, he listened, but it started to make him quite bitter inside. While the boatman continued to row the boat, the doctor asked him another question.

"Mr. Boatman. I am sure you know what astronomy is, don't you?"

"Astronomy? I don't know about those kinds of things. When the evening sky is red, that means it will be clear the next morning. When the morning sky is red, it means that the day will be cloudy. I know that much, but I don't know what astronomy is. What do you do with astronomy?"

"Haha, Mr. Boatman. Have you been rowing on this boat without even knowing what astronomy is? Mr. Boatman, three-fourths of your life is as good as dead."

Now the boatman was really offended. But because he could not say anything, he simply swallowed his anger and continued to row. Then he made a mistake. There was a rock sticking out in the middle of the river. It was a rock that he would have usually dodged very easily. But that day, he didn't see it, and the boat crashed into the rock. All of a sudden, there was a loud bang. The crash had created a hole in the middle of the boat, and river water began to flow in.

The boatman then quickly asked the doctor, "Doctor, do you know how to swim?"

"No, I don't know how to swim. What do I do?"

"What do you mean 'What do I do?' Doctor, four-fourths of your life is now sinking into the river."

People like to express the need for equality, especially politicians who are running for office. However, while the people in the world claim to want equality with their mouths, there's no one who truly desires it in their hearts. People want to be better off than others; they want to be in positions that are better and higher. They want their sons to be more successful than everyone else's sons. In actuality, they do not want equality. No matter what civilization or nation, people cry out for democracy and equality, but in actuality, people like to establish themselves in ranks and levels. They feel excitement in the fact that they are better off than others. That is a pleasure that we all feel in life. Some people bluntly boast that they are better than others. Then there are others who do not express it outwardly, but inwardly, they say to themselves, "I'm so great. I'm so smart. I can do everything well."

When people have clear thoughts in their minds that they are better than others, pride is formed. Then, they begin to despise and belittle others, believing their own thoughts to be more correct. Then they begin to live according to their own thoughts. As a result, the way they live life becomes more and more tumultuous, and it becomes more difficult for them to have relationships with other people.

He's Going to Be a Big Man in the Future! The Time of Pain Caused by that Pride

Ki Sung Kim is a man that I know very well. He grew up on a small island, and in his village they grow garlic. There was an incident that happened when he was just a student. Garlic is usually harvested during the early summer. Early in the summer of that year, the people did not take the harvested garlic home; they piled it on the curb so that they could carry it away later. However, one day, Ki Sung and his neighborhood friends stole someone's garlic at night and sold it. The person who owned the garlic reported it, and the police began an investigation. Since it was a small island village, it was quickly revealed that Ki Sung and his five friends had stolen the garlic, and they were all arrested. Six of them were put onto a boat and hauled over to a police station on the mainland. At the police station, Ki Sung thought quietly about everything. It seemed as if the punishment would be the same whether he got punished alone or if he and his friends got punished all together. So he decided to take all the blame by himself.

He spoke to the police officer that was handling the investigation saying, "Officer, to be honest with you. I am the one who said, 'Let's steal the garlic.' I prepared the cart, and I am the one who stole it. I sold the garlic, and I spent the money. My friends just followed me. They have committed no crime."

After the police checked to see if it was true, they released the five friends and only locked up Ki Sung. Ki Sung was in jail for three months. When he was released, he got on a boat to return to the island. He did not know what to do at the harbor because he thought the people of the village would be pointing fingers at him. There was a tractor that was entering the village from the harbor, so he got on for a ride. When he arrived at the village, there were some villagers having some drinks at a small store. They saw Ki Sung and applauded him. The captain of the village gave him a thumbs-up and complimented him. "Ki Sung is going to be a big man! I'm telling you. Ki Sung is a great man!"

He did not know what was going on. He later found out that throughout the village, people had heard that he had taken the full punishment for the crime and that his friends had been released. This turned a garlic thief into a hero. From then on, a new heart settled inside him: "I'm going to become a big man."

He then began to think that no matter what he did on the island, he could not become great, so he moved to Seoul. While living in Seoul, rather than becoming great, he found it difficult to even eat and get by. But because he thought he would become a big man, he didn't want to do petty things. His heart was high and arrogant, but he had hit rock bottom, and he was hungry. In the end, he became a gangster who lived using his fists, always thinking to himself, *A man only dies once, not twice. This life will end anyway, so let me live it to the fullest.*

He no longer had anything to fear, and thus, he lived a very rough life. One day, he received a tip that a rival gang was transporting a large amount of money, so he decided to steal it. With two members of his gang, he followed the car that was transporting the money. He blocked the path of the car in a deserted area and started a fight in the field. There were six people in the other gang, but they could not defeat the three of them. When the fight was over, he tried to take the bag with the cash, but the man holding the bag would not let go no matter how badly he was being beaten. Ultimately, Ki Sung stabbed this man to death and eventually went to prison for murder.

Even in prison, because Ki Sung thought he was destined to be someone great, he continually started fights and did not back down from anyone. Once, Ki Sung fought with one of the more notorious prisoners. The prison guard punished only Ki Sung and not the other prisoner. Ki Sung became so filled with anger that while he was being restrained with a rope, he kicked the guard in the face. In response, he was beaten unconscious by the mobile riot police. Ki Sung made up his mind to get revenge. While he worked burning wood in the furnace, he took one of the metal rods that was used to push the wood into the fire. After heating the rod in the fire, he broke off a piece about the length of his finger. Whenever he had time, he filed that piece of metal into a very sharp point and waited for his opportunity.

One day, in one of the hallways of the prison, he took out his new knife and held it to the prison guard's throat, saying, "This world has treated me badly, so now I don't want to live anymore. I want to go to the other world now, but it's going to be too lonely to go alone. So you're coming with me." The prison guard trembled in fear. He then dragged the prison guard into a solitary room and yelled out, "Hurry up and call the warden! Tell the attorney general to get here! Otherwise, he's dead!"

The entire prison was flipped upside down that day. After discussing how they could save the prison guard, they decided to get a pillar the size of an electrical pole and ram it into the back of the wall of the solitary confinement room. When thirty people carried that wooden pole and rammed it into the back of the wall, the wall collapsed, and Ki Sung and the prison guard were crushed under the debris. They were both knocked unconscious. Later on, he woke up, only to realize he had been beaten so badly he could not move. After this happened, there was no one who dared bother him in prison. "Now, they treat me like a human. This is how you are supposed to live life." This was the way he always lived.

After a certain period of time, inmates are transferred to other prisons. Whenever Ki Sung was transferred, if he felt a lack of respect from his fellow prisoners, he would again take a prison guard hostage. His prison sentence continued to increase, but he still did not give in. The longer the prison sentence, the worse his health became. He caught acute hepatitis and lost consciousness. The prison medical officers said that the stability of his body and mind were the most important, but since his internal organs were boiling like an active volcano, he could not be stabilized. As he lay in a small room where he couldn't even stretch out his legs, he would look at the wall, curse, laugh, and cry, and release all his rage.

There was a moment when he felt as if he were becoming mentally ill. He had at least been confident about his health, but now that his body had become sick, even though he wanted to fight, he could not fight anymore. As he found himself walking through this long tunnel of pain for the first time, he hated himself tremendously. Soon he became afraid. The pain overtook him. He had suffered tremendous amounts of pain more than most prisoners would have been able to endure. But even that pain did not cause him as much pain as the pain that he was going through now. This was a whole different kind of pain.

He asked himself, *How did I become like this?* The fact that he had entered prison at the age of twenty-three and spent his entire youth in a prison cell finally hit him. He now felt so grieved about his life. Being in there alone tormented him. *If only there is someone I could share my heart with*, he thought. *How great would it be if there was someone with whom I could have a real conversation.* His family came to mind, but it was also terribly heartbreaking to think that he would die without ever being a good son to his parents. He had never thought about this before. It was torture for him to imagine that his life would end in this solitary room, alone, where he could not be visited by anyone.

One day, there was an execution scheduled for one of the death-row inmates. The inmate pitifully resisted while being dragged away. When he looked closely, he realized that it was a death-row inmate who had fought over a cigarette butt just a day before. This inmate had been so full of his own strength. It was as if Ki Sung were looking at his own image. "That's exactly the way I'll be leaving. Why did I live like this?" He wanted to turn away from his life and find a new one. Since then, a great change occurred in Ki Sung. He has since been released and is now living a life that is completely different from the life he lived before.

People Who Live Like
the Frog in the Well

Every person, no matter who it may be, has the heart to believe in him or herself. But without thinking about it carefully, people think of themselves as really great, and they live believing only in themselves. If they would think just a little deeper, they would discover that they also have many faults and that they have also failed at many things. When they recognize this, they can begin to understand. "My thinking was all wrong. I did not do well, and I was never great. I was being deceived." When they admit this, they can clearly acknowledge who they really are.

Before people discover their true images, they think of themselves to be very smart and very good. Ki Sung Kim also lived like this. He later read the book that I wrote, *The Secret of Forgiveness of Sins and Being Born Again*. After reading the book, he said that for the first time, he was able to sincerely think about himself.

Here is another example of how dangerous it is to believe in yourself. Think about it. When you distrust someone, you check to see whether that person is telling the truth or not, but if you trust that person, you accept whatever he or she says. In the same way, a person who believes in himself does not check or double-check his thoughts; he just believes them to be correct. In reality, the thoughts of human beings are often wrong and flawed.

The thoughts that come from believing in yourself are the first level of thought. For people who remain on the first level of thought, even though they become drug addicts and live pitiful lives like Julio, they are incapable of thinking that living that way is wrong. However, if they could think just a little deeper, they would realize their thoughts are wrong. That is what we call the second level of thought. When we look at a situation from the second level of thought, we often begin to realize that the first level of thought is completely wrong. We should never just automatically follow the first-level thought that arises in our hearts. When we enter the first level of thought, we should stop and come to a different conclusion, "Let me think about it from a different angle. Are these thoughts actually correct?" We have to think about things in this way.

People who are bothered by having to think further, simply follow and act upon the first-level thoughts that arise momentarily in their minds. On the other hand, the people who know the joy of deeper thinking never end their thoughts at the first level. When they reach the second level of thought and reflect, they discover that the first-level thoughts that they once believed to be correct were actually incorrect. Yet, the people who still believe in themselves don't understand what is wrong, and without them even knowing it, they continue to live according to their own methods.

People who believe themselves to be great and despise others are this way because they have not met anyone who is greater than they are. People who think that they are smart feel that way because they haven't met someone who is smarter than they are. That is why they think the way that they do. They are like frogs in a well. The frog in the well thinks the world that it sees within the well is all there is to see. He thinks of himself as the greatest of them all. He lives this way, then one day, when he comes out of the well and sees a bull for the first time, he is shocked. The people who live in their own small worlds; the people who think of themselves to be great; and the people who think that their thoughts are right, when they are faced with difficult problems in life, can only fall into despair.

The Home of the World's Greatest Chess Player

This is a story that comes from China. An elderly man was once riding his donkey into a large city. While passing one of the houses, he saw a sign that read The Home of the World's Greatest Chess Player. The elderly man went to the door and asked for the owner of the house.

"Is there anyone home?" he called out.

"Who is it?" came a reply.

"Is this the home of the world's greatest chess player?"

"Yes, it is."

The young owner came out, saw the elderly man, and asked him, "What brings you here?"

"I live in the countryside about twenty-five miles away. I came to the city on some business, and I saw the sign on the front gate. I wanted to play a game of chess with you."

Right then, the owner laughed, and he asked him, "You want to play chess with me? You ask this even after seeing the sign?"

"Yes, it says that you play very well. So that's why I would like to play with you."

The elderly man from the countryside and the young owner, the so-called World's Greatest Chess Player, opened the chessboard, set the pieces, and sat face-to-face. The elderly man then spoke. "It's no fun to just play. Why don't we set a wager?"

"Sure, what should the wager be?"

"How about the loser gives the winner fifteen coins?"

"Agreed. Let's do that."

And the two of them began to play chess.

Since he was the greatest chess player in the world, you can imagine how skilled he must have been. The elderly man started getting pushed around. "Elderly man, checkmate!" exclaimed the young owner. The elderly man looked at the board and decided that there was no way out for him.

"I'm defeated," he said.

"That's right. You are defeated. Then as promised, you need to pay fifteen coins."

All of the sudden, the elderly man's face became red.

"I'm so sorry. What am I to do?" said the elderly man.

"Why? What do you mean?"

"I'm sorry, but I have no money."

"What? You didn't have any money, and you asked to place a wager?" The young owner had a look of confusion on his face. Then the elderly man made a proposal. "If you sell the donkey that I came here on, you can get at least fifty coins for him. Since I have been defeated, I will give you the donkey instead the money."

"That makes no sense. Elderly man, you came a long way, and you must return on that donkey. How can you return from your long journey without your donkey?" asked the young owner.

"Sure, that may be. But what am I to do? I have no money. I made a promise, so I should keep it. I would be happy if you would at least take my donkey," requested the elderly man.

"Well, that would not be polite of me."

"No, it's okay. It's okay."

"Well, if you insist, then I will take the donkey. I am very sorry."

"Please, don't feel sorry."

"Then farewell."

The elderly man handed the reins of the donkey over to the young owner, and he walked away empty-handed. How good the young owner must have felt because he won a donkey in a chess match. He changed the old saddle for a new one, and he purchased new reins. After he washed the donkey clean, he rode him around, and it made him feel very good.

However, after about a week, the elderly man returned to his house. "Sir, what brings you back here again?" asked the young owner.

"Last time, I was sorry that I could not give you the money I promised. But I was very thankful that you at least took the donkey. I came here today because I want to play another game of chess."

"But with your skill, sir, you are no match for me."

"Even so, I still want to play just one more time. This time, I have fifteen coins with me."

"Really?"

"This time, if I lose, I will give you fifteen coins, but if I win, you must return the donkey I gave you last time."

The owner was feeling good and thought, *Last time it was as if you practically gave me your donkey. Now you are here to give me fifteen coins also.*

The two of them began the chess match. However, this elderly man who was once so terrible at chess showed completely different skills in just one week. *What is this?* thought the young owner. *This elderly man is really good at chess.* The young owner was shocked. Sweat began to break out on his forehead.

After playing for a while, the elderly man said with a loud voice, "Young owner, checkmate!" There was no way out for the young owner. The man who was supposed to be the world's greatest chess player was no match for this elderly man. He was completely defeated.

"I have been defeated," said the young man.

"Then, as promised, may I take my donkey with me?"

"Sure. Of course you may."

The owner brought out the donkey. Under his ownership, the donkey had been fitted with a new saddle and reins. The donkey was now washed nice and clean. The donkey recognized the elderly man first and was very happy to see him.

"Then excuse me for all your troubles. Please be well," said the elderly man.

As he was about to mount his donkey and leave, the young owner shouted out, "Wait! I need to ask you one thing."

"What is it?"

"One week ago, sir, you were really bad at chess. But in such a short amount of time, how did you increase your skills? I'm very curious."

"Didn't I explain that to you already?"

"No, please, I'd like to know."

"I told you that I came here on some business before, right? I arrived at the city and wanted to enter into the city offices riding on the donkey. At the entrance, it was written, 'Donkeys or horses are not allowed.' So I needed a place where I could house my donkey for a week. So I purposely played chess with you. Today, I'm done with all my errands, and I need to return home. Of course, I would need my donkey, wouldn't I? That is why I won this time."

The owner was shocked. He thought he was the world's greatest chess player. This elderly man was a person who could defeat him or lose to him at will. He felt so ashamed. Immediately, he removed the sign that read The Home of the World's Greatest Chess Player from his house. I heard that from that day on, he lowered his head and became humble.

Until people meet someone greater than they are, they think of themselves as great. We may not put up a sign on the front of our gates, but in our hearts we say, "I'm good. I'm smart. I'm better than others." Everyone in this world has a small amount of that kind of heart inside of them.

As You Live, You Must Meet People Who Are Better than You, and You Must also Experience Failure

The younger son, whom I used as an example earlier, thought that he was great. He also thought that he was intelligent. Because of this, he went to a faraway country and wasted all his wealth. When a famine came to that land, he soon became hungry and only then did he realize what a foolish person he was. The younger son believed that he had something that made him better than his friends, and he truly thought of himself to be someone great. He then pressured his father into giving him a portion of his wealth. The younger son, who now had money in his hand, became very excited. He was filled with dreams of owning a grand business and succeeding. He thought that everything would go well. Before people fail, before they acknowledge the existence of those who are better than them, they think that no one else can do better.

In another story, the young man thought that he was the world's greatest chess player because he had not met anyone who was better than him. He thought that his skills were the best. However, after playing chess with the elderly man from the countryside, his belief that he could play very well was completely shattered.

As we live, we need to meet people who are greater than we are. We also need to experience failure. When the man, who thought he was the world's greatest chess player was riding on the donkey he took from the elderly man, he must have felt so boastful, strong, and arrogant. On the other hand, after being defeated by the elderly man during the rematch, when he heard the elderly man say that he lost to him the first time on purpose, he finally realized what an inadequate person he truly was.

When a person is wrong, makes mistakes, and realizes that he is much less than he thought he was, he becomes humble, sincere, and diligent. People who are still caught up in the taste of their own greatness do not listen to others and are busy putting forth their own opinions. Such people are high-hearted. They do not possess the ability to control themselves. Because of this, they fall into gambling, gaming, drugs, and they are unable to break free.

Among the many people that I have met in prison, some were people who had no other choices and ended up there. However, most of them were people who had lived believing in themselves and, as a result had fallen into sin. When you are high-hearted and believe in yourself, you can only end up failing and being destroyed. The Bible says, "Pride goes before destruction, a haughty spirit before a fall" (Proverbs 16:18). Do not just dwell on the first level of thought, thinking that you are a great person. You must realize just how much you really lack. When you transform into a humble person, your life becomes so much more rewarding.

Chapter 5

Isolation

When Hearts Do not Flow with One Another, but Are Locked Away by Themselves, Misery Is Felt

In the same way that a cellular phone would be useless if it only functioned in a house, if people's thoughts only remain within themselves, then the world of their hearts is useless. The domain of the heart needs to be broadened, but the heart to believe in one's self is what gets in the way of this.

The Single Women in America
Who Live with Their Pet Dogs

I have heard that prisoners who cause trouble can be placed in solitary confinement for several months at a time. Isn't it awful even imagining spending several months in a very small room with no one else inside? Today in this world, even though tens of millions of people live in large cities such as Tokyo, New York, Los Angeles, Paris, London, Seoul, or Beijing, their hearts are actually quite isolated. There are also many people who live alone as if they are on a deserted island. People with extremely weak hearts strongly reject doing anything that is burdensome. They prefer to spend time with people who are younger than they are and with those who they feel are more lacking. It is because they are able to deal with such people without any burden.

Not only the weak-minded, but even ordinary people prefer to be single, without any burdens. That is why I have heard that in America, there are many women who stay single after getting a divorce, but instead of getting remarried, they just live raising cats or dogs. Cats and dogs are smart compared to other animals, but they are far behind the intelligence of man. They are not picky in what they ask of their owners. If you just feed them on time and pet them every once in a while, they are satisfied. They do not argue with you or ask why you are frowning. They do not annoy you to find out why you came home late. They are just unconditionally happy to see their owners. Since cats and dogs give people a chance to have that feeling of closeness *without* the burden, many single women prefer to raise cats or dogs

In life, facing burdens occasionally is good for our mental health. If we keep avoiding burdens, our hearts become isolated. When our hearts become isolated, we enjoy being alone. We end up enjoying things that do not burden us, like computer games. When we play computer games, we can feel tension and a sense of accomplishment, which causes us to continually fall into them. The more we fall into those things, the more we want to avoid burdensome things. While we are enjoying computer games, we do not feel the beauty of people anymore. And in the end, we grow more and more disinterested in people. We become disinterested in talking with people, we become annoyed being around people, and inevitably, we become even more isolated.

The Son Who Misunderstands His Mother's Heart before Having a Conversation with Her

There are people who live isolated lives because they do not like burdens. However, there are people who magnify themselves, people who place way too much confidence in themselves, and people who do not have any exchange with others. Instead, they stubbornly exalt themselves and live isolated lives. People who think, "I am smart. I'm so great," even though they speak to other people, they think to themselves, "What do you know?" and close their hearts. So, they continue to remain isolated.

The people who cause problems in the world are people who are isolated for the most part. At KAIST University, which is known as the best university in Korea, four people committed suicide this year alone. I have never met them, but I believe that as these students were studying, they must have been people whose hearts were isolated. If these students communicated their hearts with their families, then even if they had a heart to commit suicide, they would have thought, "If I were to commit suicide, it would be so painful for my father. My mother would be terribly sad. My brother would be so disappointed in me." With these thoughts in mind, they would not have been able to put their intentions into action. The first time I provided suicide prevention training on the military bases in Korea, I thought long and hard over what I would speak about to the soldiers. First, I analyzed their hearts in order to see what kinds of people committed suicide. The special trait of people who commit suicide is that their hearts are truly isolated. Therefore, when a certain thought enters their minds, they become caught up in it, and believe that it is right.

This story that I am going to tell you is a true story. During the Korean War, many soldiers died in the fight between North Korea and South Korea. When the fighting was at its fiercest, there was a woman who was living in Los Angeles. One night, around midnight, her home phone rang. She answered the phone, and said, "Hello?"

"Mom? It's me, John."

She was shocked. John was her only son, and he was fighting in the Korean War. She always became very anxious when she heard about the news of how many American soldiers were dying in the war. But now, she was receiving this phone call from her son.

"Is this really you, John?" she asked.

"Yes, Mother, it's me," John replied.

"Where are you right now?"

"I just arrived at the Los Angeles airport."

"Really? How's your health?"

"I am fine, and I am healthy."

The woman was so happy. She said, "John, thank you so much for being alive. Now, hurry up and come home."

"Mother, I am with my friends right now, but I will come home tomorrow morning."

"All right then, I will be waiting for you. Please come home quickly."

His mother was about to hang up the phone, but John continued to talk.

"Mother, there's a friend that I want to bring home with me."

"Sure. Bring him over. Who is he?"

"He's a friend I fought together with in the war. He stepped on a landmine on the battlefield, so he is missing a leg, an arm, and he has lost an eye as well."

"Oh, how terrible! Sure, let him come over and enjoy himself and get some good rest at our house for about a week. Then we can let him go home."

"Mother, I was hoping that I could live the rest of my life with this friend of mine."

"What are you talking about? I guess the war has made you extremely sentimental. Think about it. He's missing an arm and a leg, so how is he going to use the restroom? How is he going to take a shower? If you live with this kind of person for a long time, it will eventually become extremely uncomfortable for you. Later on, you will become irritated with such an arrangement. Just let him stay for a little while, and let him go home."

"But Mother, I need to live with this friend. Can't he just come and live with me?"

"I'm sure that on the battlefield you may have such emotions, but when you actually see the reality of the situation, it's not going to be the way you imagined. It will be best if you send him home later on."

"Okay, Mother."

"It's the right thing to do."

"Mother."

"Yes?"

"Please take care of yourself."

"Why are you saying goodbye? Just hurry up and come home."

"Mother?"

"What, son?"

"Mother, please be healthy. Okay?"

"Okay. Hurry up and come home."

She hung up the phone, completely overwhelmed by the fact that her son, who had gone to war, had made it back alive. She quickly went into her son's room, and cleaned and organized it. She could not fall asleep. She then took out the iron and began to iron her son's clothes nicely and neatly. She then hung them up in his closet and she placed flowers next to his bed. Her happiness could not be expressed in words. It had been such a long time since she had felt this kind of happiness. She went to the kitchen and began to cook the food she wanted to give her son. Sunrise was still a long way off, but as she waited for her son, she was filled with nothing but joy as she cooked for him. Finally, day began to break. Time passed. Eight in the morning, then nine in the morning but her son still had not come home. The woman was dying inside because she wanted to see her son so badly. "What is this boy doing? Why has he not come home?" First 10 o'clock, then 11 o'clock, but still, her son had not come home. "These young boys are so busy hanging out with their friends; they must have lost their minds." It became noon, and at 1 o'clock in the afternoon, she heard the phone ring. "Why is this boy not coming home and calling me again?" she thought and picked up the phone.

"Hello?" she answered. It was the voice of a stranger.

"Excuse me, is this John's house?"

"Yes, it is."

"Are you John's mother?"

"Yes, I am. Who is this?"

"This is the police. Your son jumped to his death from his hotel room. We need you to come quickly to the hospital as soon as you can."

The woman thought she was dreaming. "My son who had just returned from the battlefield is dead? What is this?" She could not believe it was all real. She'd had a difficult time believing that her son was alive and back in the first place, but now, "My son who said he would be home soon, is dead?" The woman drove her car as fast as she could to the hospital. The police were waiting for her. They guided her to a room in the hospital. There was a solitary bed in the room. A man was lying on top of the bed completely covered in a white sheet.

The police removed the sheet and the woman was shocked. The person lying on the bed was surely her loving son, John. But he was missing one eye, and his face was filled with scars. He was also missing an arm and a leg. The lady held her dead son and cried, "John! John! Why didn't you tell me that it was you? Why didn't you tell your mother that it was you?"

As a part of the UN Forces, John fought in the Korean War and on the eastern battlefields; he stepped on a landmine in the middle of a battle. Fortunately, he did not die instantly, but he was severely wounded. The medics took John, who was unconscious, and transported him to a hospital. When John regained his consciousness and recovered, he tried to move his legs, but he had no feeling in one of them. He looked down and he could not see one of his legs. He was missing an arm, and he had lost an eye as well. John was then moved to the hospital in Okinawa, Japan where he continued to receive treatment and was eventually sent back to America. On the flight to Los Angeles, John fell into deep thought. "When I left, I left healthy. But now I am returning a cripple. When I arrive in America with this body, will my friends like me?" Even in his own eyes, he looked so scary and ugly. It seemed as if his friends would not like him this way. Tom, Matthew, Andrew; one by one, as he thought of his friends, it seemed as if not one of them would welcome him home or be happy to see him. It was apparent that his girlfriend would dislike him even more. John finally thought about his mother. "No matter what anyone else says in this world, Mother will surely still love me." But as he looked at himself, he lost all his courage again. "No, how could my mother like me? This is what I have become. My mother may not even be able to love me."

After he came out of the airport, John wanted to know his mother's heart, so he gave her a phone call. "Mother, I have a friend. This friend stepped on a landmine on the battlefield. He's missing an arm and a leg, and he only has one eye left. I want to live the rest of my life with this friend. I have to live the rest of my life with him."

But his mother's voice that he heard over the phone was cold. "Hey, you have become sentimental since you have gone to the war. Think about it. How is he going to use the bathroom if he is missing an arm and a leg? How is he going to shower? You are going to become irritated and uncomfortable staying with him. Afterwards, you are going to feel burdened. Let him stay with you for a while, and then send him home."

Upon hearing those words, John misjudged his mother's heart. "I will be a burden to my mother. Mother will be irritated with me. Mother will become uncomfortable with me. If that's the case, there is not a single person who will want to receive me. Then, what is the point of living?" Ultimately, John chose to kill himself. His mother, on the other hand, clung to her son who had died this way, crying out, "John! Why didn't you tell me that it was you? If you had lost an arm and a leg, I would have become your arm. I would have become your leg. It would have been such an honor for me."

People Today Who Hide Their Hearts and Speak only with Words

Even between the mother and son who had been apart for a long time, they were unable to give and receive their hearts to each other. The son was unable to figure out the true heart of his own mother. He sincerely wanted to figure out what his mother's heart was, but he misunderstood her heart. Conflicts often arise in this world because we do not know each other's hearts. People need to have lots of conversations with one another. You can tell immediately, just by looking at a person, whether he is tall or short, or whether he has a handsome or ugly face. But there is no one who can see the heart. "I was so happy to see you today. I am so sorry about yesterday. You know, after thinking about it, I realize that I really hurt you last time." This tool called, *language,* is necessary to express our hearts; hearts which are unseen by couples, siblings, friends, by teachers and their students. As people speak and exchange words with one another, they can know and feel each other's hearts. "Oh, that was why he behaved like that." "It must have been so difficult for him at that time." When you know the heart of one another, you can truly understand each other. You can believe in each other, and you can flow together with the same heart. However, sometimes, we say things that are not actually in our hearts. Rather than express what is exactly in our hearts, we prefer to hide what is in our hearts, so we beat around the bush by having conversations with just words. But saying things that are not truly in our hearts is no different from lying. In actuality, it is deceiving the other person. This blocks hearts from flowing into one another. When we know each other's hearts, like electricity that flows through electrical wires, people become happy when they know each other's hearts and their hearts naturally flow into one another. On the other hand, when our hearts do not flow together, we become miserable.

John tried to discover his mother's heart using foolish methods. He should have honestly said what was in his heart. "Mother, I lost one of my arms, one of my legs, and one of my eyes on the battlefield. Will you still love me? If you don't want me, then I won't come home." However, he spun his words around, saying, "I have this friend…" That served as the obstacle that blocked his mother's heart from flowing into his. And because John did not know of his mother's love, he chose to commit suicide. If he had precisely known his mother's heart, he would have never done such a thing.

Many times, the hearts of parents and children are not able to flow together because of the generation gap. Most fathers compare their sons' lives to the lives that they have lived. That is why there are many things that seem unsatisfactory to them. As a result, they often say things that are worrisome. According to his son, rather than sounding like a show of concern, his parents' words sound annoying and intrusive. This only causes the son to feel frustrated, and makes him want to rebel. When this happens over and over again, the father and son grow further and further apart.

When I give a task to my son, I don't just give him the task. There is a school in Huntington, New York that our mission operates. During the early stages of the founding of this school, the person who was appointed to be the first president did not properly understand the mind-set behind the establishment of the school. We explained it to him several times, but the operations of the school did not go well at all. Ultimately, he quit and the licensure of the school which was pending at the time, became a problem that was then given to my son. "Why don't you go to New York for ten days and take care of this." After I explained the work that needed to be done, I explained my heart in detail about why I wanted to do this work. "This is the heart with which I started the school in New York. However, the school has not been run according to my heart. This is the kind of school that I want to build in the future. I am too busy, so I am unable to go there. Please go instead of me and get this done." I not only directed him to work, but I continually instilled in him the deep heart of why I wanted to do this. When my son works knowing his father's heart, it is as if I am there doing the work. Then when the work is done, I am satisfied and my son is also full of joy.

Just as Idle Water Spoils, the Heart also Becomes Diseased When It Is Isolated

When there is no conversation between parents and their children, and the only words that are spoken are about each other's discomfort, they only grow further and further apart. This is also true between a husband and wife. When they do not have conversations with one another, and when they end up only speaking when they are angry, their conversations are only filled with complaints. Emotions arise that only end up causing them to grow further and further apart. When parents speak to their children, they should not only speak about the outcomes such as, "Why do you only play computer games and refuse to study?", "Why do you always waste money?", or "Why do you wear those kinds of clothes?" Parents should express what is in their hearts. "Are these the kinds of clothes people your age like? Wow, the times have changed so much. When I was your age, I could never wear these kinds of clothes. So that is how you do things. I used to do things like this…"

Sometimes, you also have to give your children sincere advice about life. "I farm here every year. Even though it is tough, the harvest time in the fall makes me feel so happy.

When your grandfather was raising me, our country was very poor. Your grandfather often went hungry so that he could feed me. At that time, I had no idea what he did for me. Now that we are better off, I can actually buy you whatever you want to eat, and that makes me so happy, son."

Sometimes, you have to tell your children about the relationship between you and your spouse. "When I first married your mother and we began to live together, we fought a lot. Your mother's personality is quite different from mine. But as we continued to live together, over time, our hearts became similar to one another."

When the father says what is exactly inside his heart, then his son can open his heart to his father. He will then think to himself, "That was how my dad lived. This is what my dad liked. If I do this, then my dad will be happy."

As their hearts flow this way, they can then have real conversations with one another.

"Father, I want to stop playing games, but it's not working out as I wanted."

"I understand. That's how all people are, son. That's why you shouldn't try to just stop yourself from playing games, but you have to look for something that gives you even more joy. For example, try sports or something else. When you want to play computer games, try turning your heart towards something else, and then I think it will get better. When I used to have my bad habit a long time ago, that's what I used to do."

This is the way that hearts must flow with one another. Hearts should not be blocked off from one another. When a person's heart is not dwelling in just one place, and when the entire family's heart flows together, then people can be happy. Then, even though you may not ride in fancy cars or eat fancy food, but when your heart transforms in this way and flows together, that is the definition of true happiness. Misery arises mostly when people's hearts do not flow with one another. Sometimes, we go through difficulties that are inevitable. However, the cause of most problems is the discord that is caused by the disruption of the flow of the heart.

Surely, I Have Chosen You, but Why Can't You Trust Me?

There is a woman I know who, before getting married, was beautiful, had grown up in a great family, and was very well educated. She reached the age to get married, and saw her older sisters marrying men who had the best circumstances in the world, but her sisters' marriages always ended in divorce. She felt very resentful about the institution of marriage. Then one day, she saw a young, crippled man in the village that she lived in. As she saw this man limping, this young woman suddenly thought to herself, "I wonder what it would be like for me to marry that man. If I were to marry that man, that man he would be happy. If my husband were happy then I, too, would be happy. So what if he is crippled? So what if we are poor? All we need is happiness. What more would we need?"

One day, she told her mother, "Mother, I want to get married."

"Really? Is there a man you've set your sights on?"

"Yes!"

Her daughter, who was usually not interested in marriage, was now all of a sudden speaking about marriage. Her mother had an expression of joy on her face, but became curious.

"Who is he? Where does he live?"

Her daughter then began to explain about the man she was intending to marry. Her mother was stunned, frightened, and horrified. "Are you out of your mind? What is it you lack that you would want to marry a cripple like him? Out of the question! Not only is he that way, but his family is also as poor as poor can be. I cannot allow you to marry into that family."

"Mother, what are you talking about? If we are happy, then isn't that enough?"

"Happiness, whatever! No way!"

But this young woman's heart was steadfast. Even though her mother tried to bully her, and her father tried to firmly dissuade her, she would not budge an inch. "Mother, I've made a decision. Even great people get divorced, but I want to marry this man and I am going to become his legs. Then we will truly be happy. If my husband is happy, then wouldn't I also be happy? No matter what anyone else says, he's the one I am going to marry."

She went to that man's house and revealed her heart to his parents. "I want to marry your son."

Even the young man's family was extremely shocked.

"No, our son is unhealthy, and our family is very poor. You are very pretty and from a well-to-do family. How could this marriage work?"

That was what they told her, but the young man's parents were so happy to hear these words come from this young woman. Despite the strong opposition, the two of them were married. However, no one from the bride's family attended the wedding, and after getting married, she lived with her new husband's family. Her parents-in-law were so thankful to her that they cared for her with all their hearts. The husband was also so good to her that it was impossible for her to be treated any better. This woman felt as though she was living in a dream. She was so happy that she felt like a princess in an enchanted forest. Her parents-in-law were happy, her husband was happy, and ever day was like living in a dream.

After a few months had passed, her mother-in-law told her, "Darling, starting from today, why don't you go into the markets and buy the food and groceries?" Then she gave her the money and the shopping basket. Until now, she had only stayed at home, but now she was able to go out, and this also made her happy. As she shopped around in the market, she bought vegetables, fish and a few more groceries with a joyful heart, and came home a little late.

But her husband was angry. "Where have you been all this time?"

"At the market." The wife answered as if it was nothing.

"You, get in here!"

"Why? What's wrong?"

"Who did you see in the market today?"

"Who did I see? I didn't see anyone."

"How dare you lie? You really didn't see anyone?"

"No, I only saw the mackerel vendor."

The wife could not understand why her husband was acting this way. He kept asking her, "Who did you meet?" But when she answered she had not met anyone, he snapped back at her, shouting, "Why are you lying?" The husband continued to ask angrily, then opened the door of the room. Near the door to the room, was a charcoal furnace, and next to the furnace, were tongs used to handle the charcoal. The husband then picked up the tongs and ruthlessly beat his wife. Even as she was being beaten, she could not understand why her husband was acting this way. After her husband beat her for a while, he seemed to come back to senses. He told his wife that he was very sorry. He held his wife and cried and begged her to forgive him. He then put medication on the cuts and bruises where he had beaten her with the tongs. From that day on, this woman's happiness was shattered into little pieces. Even while cooking or talking, she would become dazed and blankly fall into her thoughts. Her smile completely disappeared from her face. Even though the husband knew his wife was not up to anything, he would always become caught up in strange thoughts every time she went out.

"My wife is so pure. That is why she married a person like me. But one day, when she meets some handsome man, she's going to throw me away and leave me." Whenever he would imagine this, he could not bear it. No matter how much the husband thought, "I should stop thinking like this. I shouldn't be imagining these things," the thoughts would come to his mind and drive him crazy. As he remained in that kind of pain, when his wife would return home, he would beat her again with the tongs. Then, he would once again say that he was sorry, and beg for forgiveness. He would beg and cry for her forgiveness, but eventually, she decided to speak to her husband and to her mother and father-in-law.

"I have decided today to leave this home. When I decided that I wanted to marry my husband, my parents tried so hard to stop me, but I loved my husband. I thought my husband would be happy if I became his legs, and I believed that if my husband were happy, then that would make me happy. However, my husband has become even more miserable since he married me. He's always insecure and afraid because of me."

To her husband, she said, "Surely, I chose you, but why don't you trust me?"

People who remain in an isolated world for a long time are unable to break free from some of the thoughts that enter their minds. It is the same as falling into a whirlpool; no matter how well you swim, you cannot break free. No matter how much they think, "I shouldn't act this way," they are unable to break free from that thought. They do not accept other people's warnings and advice, but only listen to them superficially. So, they are not effective.

The crippled husband said to himself, "I shouldn't act this way," but every time his wife went out, in his mind, she would eventually meet another man. She would hold hands with some other man. She would follow that man and go someplace far away. Even though it was not real and only in his imagination, he was unable to break free from those thoughts, and therefore, he felt unbearable pain. He beat his wife, and ultimately, he ended up losing her.

If You Cannot Share Your Heart with a Person When You Feel Lonely, How Can That Be a Person You Love?

We must search our own hearts to see whether they are isolated or not. It is a problem to think that you are great, but when you despise others and end up cutting off conversations, then you have to remember that this is what causes you to be isolated. No matter who a person may be, if that person is isolated, then he cannot be free from the frame of his own thoughts.

Once, when I was in Jeonju Prison, I met a woman who had killed her husband and daughter. This woman committed these terrible crimes after being isolated inside of her own thoughts. We can tell how scary it is to be unable to break free from our thoughts when we listen to the story of this woman.

It all started after this woman gave birth to her daughter in the hospital and was returning home. I've heard that after women give birth, their bodies become exhausted, and their hearts also become very weak. One day, her husband went to work, and she was lying with her baby at home. All of a sudden, a fearful thought entered her heart. She was afraid somebody would break in to her home, so she locked all the windows. However, her fear did not disappear.

When her husband came home in the evening, she said, "Honey, I'm so scared." Her husband heard these words, but he did not look into the heart of his wife who was so afraid.

"What are you scared of? This is our home. Do you think there are monsters here? Everything is fine. Don't be afraid," he told her.

The next day, he went to work as usual. The man's wife was so afraid of being in the house alone that she took her baby and went outside. She saw a taxi and mindlessly got in. The driver asked, "Where do you want to go?" She asked the driver to take her to Dajeon where her parents lived. It is 70 km from Jeonju to Dajeon, but she took the taxi and went to her parent's house. When she arrived, she got out of the taxi, and right then, her older brother, who was coming home, saw her. He could not understand why his little sister, who just delivered a new baby, would come so far.

"Why are you here?" her brother asked. "Are you out of your mind, going out like this with a newborn baby?" Her older brother loudly scolded her. She could not say anything. When her older brother saw her standing there, unable to say anything, he yelled at her again. "Hurry up and go home!"

So she left and returned home, sobbing while holding her baby in her arms. She lay down in her room, but the heart of fear kept coming to her. And each time this woman became afraid, there was no one with whom she could share her heart. She fell deeper and deeper into her fears. She eventually concluded, "If I continue like this, then I'm going to die." That is how she spent each and every day. She had no idea what would actually happen if she died. "If I die, my husband will probably marry another woman. Then that woman will sleep with my husband on our bed. She will probably use my closet, too." Thinking such thoughts made her so sorrowful. "When that woman moves in, she will hate my daughter for being the daughter of his first wife." She then began to imagine all sorts of things. "In the cold winter, she will send my daughter outside. And when she kicks my daughter out, she will stay in this warm house, laughing and having a great time. Then my daughter will be knocking on the door, yelling, 'Mother, it's cold! Please open the door!'"

When she thought about that, she wept and wailed. Although she was not yet dead, her husband had not remarried, and her baby was not being abused by an evil stepmother, all of these thoughts had become reality. While having these kinds of thoughts, she looked at her newborn baby, and thought, "You are better off dead than to live that kind of a life. Rather than live a life of being abused by your stepmother, I will let you die." Her heart flowed in this nonsensical direction.

A certain strength that she could not see with her eyes was dragging her, and she could clearly feel it. Her thoughts continued to go on even further. "Since my husband is going to marry another woman and abuse my daughter, he also deserves to die!" That evening, as her husband was opening the door to enter into the house with some snacks that he had bought for his wife; she stood behind him, and stabbed him to death with a knife. Then she stabbed and killed her daughter. She tried to kill herself and began stabbing herself all over her body. Her entire body was terribly damaged.

People must have someone to share their hearts with. Whether they are in fear, or whether they experience times of difficulty, sadness, or joy, people need someone to share their hearts with. That is why you need true friends. That is why you need family. That is also why you need a person to love. If you cannot share your heart with a friend or a family member when you are sad, then how can that person be a friend or family member? If you cannot share your heart with a person when you feel lonely, how can that be a person you love?

Suppose there were a flood and your house was carried away. You could rest for a few days at your friend's house, or at the home of a loved one. The world of the heart is also the same. Having someone to share your heart with when you feel insecure, scared, or afraid, that becomes strength to overcome your difficulties. You must live with your heart opened to one another so that even though your thoughts may flow in the wrong direction, you can be freed from them. I've seen many college students who have been isolated inside the wrong thoughts, whose hearts changed through conversation, which led to changes in the direction of their lives. When we open and share our hearts with one another, we can stop misery.

Chapter 6

Exchange

If There Is a Problem You Cannot Solve, It Is because You Are Trying to Solve It on Your Own

When you do not have the power to solve a problem on your own, struggling with it will not make the problem go away. You need to accept the hearts of other people. Since your heart is not always precise, through accepting the hearts of others, you can become free from your isolated thoughts.

A Problem Cannot Be Solved by You Trying to Solve It on Your Own

The struggles of college students are quite simple, but they become serious when the students struggle by themselves. Every year, the International Youth Fellowship holds World Camps in many different countries. At first they were only held in Korea, but as the years progressed, they were held in Kenya, Ghana, Peru, and Mexico. The World Camp is spreading to other countries as an event for college students all over the world. Many times I have seen young people who have attended the World Camp change into completely different people by the time the World Camp ends. Leaders from many different nations who wanted to unite with us in our cause have enthusiastically sponsored us. Ministers, prime ministers, and even presidents have come to our camps and encouraged the young people. We are currently receiving proposals from the governments of the nations where the World Camp has not yet been held. They are aggressively trying to host the World Camp.

One of the main reasons we hold the World Camps is to provide a place where students who are isolated, have problems, or have stopped communicating can exchange with other students and with teachers. When we have such sessions, the hearts of many students automatically change. On average, about 3,000 people attend a World Camp, and we divide students into male and female classes. Our activities are primarily held within classes. There are about ten students per class, and each class has a teacher who is in charge. The students in a class get together to share what they have held in their hearts. As they share and reveal their problems and difficulties, and talk to one another, they begin to change. At first they are embarrassed, but when they begin to bring out and share their problems, even those that are difficult to talk about are resolved. The struggles that college students have are not issues that require a great deal of concern, but when they keep everything to themselves, oftentimes, that nurtures and heightens the problems. However, since college students are much more pure-hearted than adults, even though their problems may appear to be complicated, when you analyze them, there are only about three or four causes of their problems. However, there are many students who struggle with their problems alone, and reach a point of no return.

For example, there are incidences of rape among female students. Consider how much rage they must possess, and how painful it must be to have experienced such a thing. What woman would not be tormented after having her purity trodden upon? Unfortunately, because rape is something shameful to its victims, it is not something they can speak to other people about. When they experience such a thing, women who are able to have their hearts flow with another person can curse that man in their hearts and then erase it from their hearts. They can say, "That man deserves to die," and go about their lives. Sure, they won't be able to just quickly forget everything, but they are not bound by their thoughts, and they continue to strive to live their lives. On the other hand, some students are unable to break free from this kind of incident, so they remain in turmoil. Thoughts of fear enter and they begin to lock their doors. Some even start to wear layers and layers of underwear. Even when they see a man walking by, they think that he might try to hurt them, and they become afraid.

The Thought of a Young Woman Who Thought She Could not Be Married because She Thought She Was Sexually Disabled

Once, a young lady came from a long distance to have a counseling session with me. I could tell that her heart had become severely weakened, and while I tried to understand why that was, I just could not figure it out. She was twenty eight years old at the time, and I mentioned that it would be good for her to get married. People differ from person to person, but in certain cases like this, a person may change when she receives the love from her husband, and comes to rely on him in her heart. However, when I suggested this to her, the expression on her face became very serious and she said that she should absolutely never get married. "What do you mean you should never get married? Whether it is a woman or a man, when it's the right time, they can get married. So what do you mean you shouldn't get married?"

"I just shouldn't."

"What are you talking about? Why shouldn't you get married?"

"Because I am sexually handicapped, I cannot have a good marriage."

I was wondering what she meant. To me it seemed that there was no clear reason for this, and that she was only considering herself to be sexually disabled in her thoughts. I asked some of the ladies there to take her to a gynecologist and have her examined to see if she could have a normal marriage. After a gynecologist examined her, he said that she was completely normal and had no problems at all. He said that if she got married it would be perfectly fine for her to have children. However, she continued to believe with great assurance that she was sexually handicapped. The reason I sent her to the hospital was to have her hear from a doctor that she was not sexually handicapped, and to free her from that thought.

Upon returning from the hospital, she accused the doctor and me of making up her diagnosis.

"I was at home," I assured her.

"No, you could've told the doctor what to do over the phone," she replied.

"Let me ask you just one thing. Why don't you go to a different city and go to a gynecologist I know nothing about and get yourself examined there? That doctor will also say that you are normal. You have no problems. You are fine. You can have a normal marriage. If you meet a good husband, you will become happy."

"No, I am sexually handicapped, and I should not get married."

That young woman refused to listen to anyone else and chose to only believe in her own thoughts. That was exactly the state she was in when she left, and I have not heard what happened to her since.

Once, a man in his forties came to see me, telling me that he had AIDS. Then I asked him how he came to know that he had AIDS. He then told me about the kind of life he had lived. He had been a sailor for a long time and when his ship would arrive at a harbor, prostitutes would get onboard the ship and they would stay with the sailors for days at a time. That was how promiscuously he lived. He told me that his symptoms are exactly like those of an AIDS patient. I told him to go to the hospital first in order to get an accurate test done. Soon afterwards, he came to me and said, "Pastor, I got myself tested, and they said I don't have AIDS." He was always so afraid of confirming that he had AIDS that he was too afraid to get himself tested. He could not tell anyone else about this, and he struggled with the thought of living as an AIDS patient. In this manner, whenever he would fall into his isolated thoughts, he could not break free from them.

When You Are Led through Conversation Instead of Trying to Solve Problems Yourself, Even Problems of the Heart Become Easy

Let me give you just one more example. I met a female student who had some problems during the World Camp. She also only believed in her thoughts. "Pastor, just leave me alone. It's not going to work. I have received counseling many times, but it doesn't work." I spoke to her for 30 minutes about life. She just listened quietly. I could feel that she was listening to my words with her heart.

When we have problems, instead of straining ourselves to try and take care of them, it is much better for us to take care of that problem with someone else. If a person who does not know how to swim is straining to get out of the water, if someone on the side of the pool or by the shore pulls him just a little, then he is able to come out from the water very easily. Even when we have certain problems in our hearts, when we strain with all our might to solve them on our own, it is very difficult. However, through conversation, if someone else leads our hearts just a little, then it becomes extremely easy. At that moment it is most important to receive the words of other people into our hearts.

Many college students who had fallen into a number of problems in their lives simply accepted my words into their hearts, and I can see them changing so clearly. Once they accepted those words into their hearts, they changed very easily, without straining. When I spoke to that female student about life, I could feel that she was accepting my words with her heart. "She's going to change," I thought to myself. I ended my talk with her that day, and said, "Today, I am a little busy, so I will wrap it up here. But when you have time tomorrow, come here again, and I will discuss this with you in further detail. If you don't want to come, you don't have to. Do whatever you like, but I will make time for you tomorrow. So if you want, come here."

The following evening, after I stepped down from finishing the Mind Lecture session, that female student was right there, waiting for me. I began to talk with her.

"Are your parents divorced?" I asked.

"Yes."

"Do you know what happens when parents with college-aged daughters like you get divorced?"

"What happens?"

"The father tries to make you take his side, and the mother tries to make you take her side, no matter what. Therefore, both of them will try not to upset you, and they will try to cater to you as much as possible. They will not rebuke you even if you do something wrong, and they will only say good things and things that you want to hear. Therefore, when you become frustrated with your mother, you can just go to your father, and when you become uncomfortable staying with your father, you can just go to your mother. In that way, you live doing whatever you want. So there is no one who can provide the correct structure for you. That's what is making you miserable."

I explained this to her in more detail. After listening for a while, she burst into tears. "That's right, Pastor," she said. "What you said is right. That is exactly how I live because both of my parents love me. When I would stay with my mother, after a while, I would become full of complaints, so I would just go to my father. And when I would get bored with staying with my father, I would go back to my mother. That is how I have lived. There is no one who leads my actions. I live doing whatever I want, and that is why I have become a stubborn, problematic child."

"Who said that you are a problem? No, you are not a problematic child. You just need to open your heart. When you first saw me, you told me not to say anything to you and to just leave you alone. You said that counseling is not going to work. That was what you thought. Things did not work out for you because you were following the thought that things were not going to work out. Now open your heart for once and listen to the words I am saying; then you will change." From that day on, I saw her changing, having conversations with her friends, and smiling brightly.

There is no crude oil in Korea. That is why we have to buy it at expensive prices from other countries in order for us to operate the tens of millions of cars here. Without purchasing the oil, there's no way for us to get fuel. If you do not have your own crude oil, you have to buy it. It is the same with taking care of problems of the heart. If you do not have the power to overcome the problems that you have, then why should you struggle to solve those problems on your own. You must receive the heart of another person. The reason for this is that your thoughts are not always correct. In other words, your thoughts may be wrong. But if you do not have conversations with other people, then you will continue to think that your incorrect thoughts are correct, and then you will settle and live the rest of your life in that state. Contrarily, no matter who you are, you can break free from your isolated thoughts through accepting the words of others.

Do not Turn the Lights On! Remove the Strap from Your Hats, and Throw Them All Down to the Ground

There are specific thoughts that people have, when they are at the first level. The first level of thought is the immediate response that arises when a person faces a particular problem or situation. At this level, people believe in themselves and they believe that their thoughts are right. But once you look at this first level of thought from a different angle, then the second level of thought arises. The second level of thought is higher and has more depth. When a person does not stop at the second level of thought but thinks about it yet again from another perspective, he can then move to a more mature third level of thought. In this way, when a person continues to repeat this process by continually entering the second and third levels of thought, he gets to a point where he realizes that his first level of thought was impulsive and incorrect. The more he thinks about it, the healthier his thoughts become.

In China during the Chu dynasty, King Jang won the war and the country was at peace. He wanted to praise the efforts of his commanders who had put their lives on the line and suffered for the nation. In order to commend them, he threw a grand party. In the king's plaza, candles were lit and a party was thrown. As his commanders had one drink, then two drinks, they became very relaxed and happy. They were beginning to have a lot of fun, and King Jang was also very happy.

Suddenly, the wind blew out all the candles at the banquet. In the middle of that darkness, his concubine, who had been sitting next to him, suddenly screamed, "Ah!" and then she yelled out, "Your Highness, someone has come and kissed me on my lips." All of the king's subjects began mumbling to each other and chaos began to ensue. "How much could this person have drunk that he dares to kiss the King's concubine in front of the King?" The concubine once again yelled out, "My King, I have pulled the strap off of his hat. So, please hurry and turn the lights on, and capture the man who has a strap missing from his hat. May that criminal be cut into pieces!"

All of a sudden, the feast fell silent, and King Jang was overflowing with rage. "How dare someone do such a thing in my presence? Hurry up and capture this person and kill him." However, when he thought about it a little more, another thought came to him,

"Today, I am giving this party to bring joy to my loyal servants who have served this nation. If I capture that subject and punish him, then what is the point of having this feast?" Then, he thought about it one more time,

I, too, have made mistakes when I was drunk. This person was drunk and that is why he did what he did when the lights went out. This is entirely possible. He did not intentionally commit this crime; he must have done this because he was overcome with drunkenness and captivated by the beauty of my concubine.

Just a little while before, King Jang had been caught up in his first level of thought, thinking that the servant who did this should immediately be captured and executed. But, when he thought about it again, he began to believe that he should not punish that servant.

The king spoke, "Everyone!"

"Yes, Your Highness."

"Do not turn the lights on."

"What?"

At the command of King Jang, the party once again became solemn. King Jang continued, "Everyone, listen. Remove the straps from your hats and throw them to the ground. If you do not do this, then you will not be able to avoid punishment. Understood?"

"Yes, Your Highness!"

"Has everyone removed and thrown down the straps from their hats and thrown them to the ground?"

"Yes, Your Highness!"

"Check one more time. Has everyone thrown them down?"

"Yes, we have, Your Majesty."

"Now turn on the lights."

All the candles at the banquet were lit once again, and King Jang and all his subjects continued to drink and party joyfully, as if nothing had happened. Time had passed, and three years later, the Chu dynasty faced a great danger. The neighboring Jin dynasty brought their soldiers for an invasion. Because the enemy's strength was so vicious, there was no one to stop them. Right then, one of King Jang's commanders came forward and said, "Your Majesty, allow your servant to go and destroy the enemy with his whole life." King Jang was so pleased that he could not speak. That commander then took his men and fought, putting his life on the line. A person who fights with a heart, ready to die, cannot be overcome. Because he was attacking with his life on the line, the soldiers of the Jin dynasty, who were filled with confidence, had their morale broken. Then they began to flee. The Chu dynasty had won the victory. After winning the war, the commander came before the king, knelt down and bowed.

The king could not overcome his joy and told the commander to rise. "You have saved this nation. I will give you a great reward," the king said.

But the commander said something strange.

"Your Majesty, may you kill me now."

"What? What do you mean? You did not care for your own life and you have brought salvation to your nation, and now you are asking me to kill you? How unfitting those words are? Surely, I will bestow a great reward unto you."

"No, Your Majesty, your servant is deserving of death."

"What do you mean?"

"Three years ago at the feast in the king's plaza, Your Majesty's concubine looked so beautiful in the eyes of your drunken servant that I went and kissed her on the lips. That day, your servant was supposed to die, but Your Majesty has kept him alive. Afterwards, I thought about this regretful action, and I have wanted to die several times, but I thought, 'I cannot just die without repaying the King for his grace.' For this long, I have been waiting for an opportunity to repay that grace. Today was the opportunity that the heavens have given me. Therefore, it was only fitting that I go forward and fight, putting my life on the line. And through the help of the heavens, I was able to win the battle. Now, I have no more regrets remaining. So, now may you put your servant to death."

King Jang took his commander by the hand and stood him up. "Thank you, General. Thank you so much! Indeed, you have saved our nation, and you have saved me."

When You Go Beyond Your First Level of Thought, You Obtain the Ability to Think and Develop

This story, which comes from the proverb, entitled, *Cheol Young Ji Yeon*, which means the party where the hat strap was removed, illustrates the great difference between the results of the first level of thought and that of second level thinking. Because many people today do not want to think deeply, they do not experience having second level thoughts. Therefore, they end up following their mediocre judgment. Through that, they go through pain that they did not have to go through. When you think more deeply about certain things, you are able to be more discreet with your decisions.

People with isolated hearts remain at the first level of thought. Because it is difficult for them to have the second level of thought, they simply finish everything at the first level. Then they become regretful because they finished things that way. I have done church construction many times, and after finishing the construction, I would often think, "It would've been better to have done this to the ceiling, and it would have been better to have done this to the glass." Then the next time we build a church building, I reflect upon the regrets of the previous construction experience, and begin the new construction with that in mind. Even so, upon finishing, other regrets still remain and I think, "I should've done this like that." The more we think, the more we come to realize that we should not just do things according to the first level of thought.

People who believe in themselves end up making mistakes and going through difficulties because they finish everything at their first level of thought. If King Jang had just stopped at his first level of thought, then that commander would have died, and as a result, the nation and its future would have fallen into great difficulty. However, King Jang did not act according to the first level of thought; he thought deeper about it. He was then able to gain more desirable results. As we continue to think more about things, we can come to the conclusion, "I thought wrong. If I continue following what I first thought, then I will be in great trouble." Then we transform into people who can be free from bad situations. Life advances because people think deeply. We must think deeply. The more we think deeply, the better our thoughts become.

Chapter 7

Change

The Heart Begins to Open When We Receive Love

Once people are loved, you begin to open your heart. A person who does not interact with other people is isolated and falls into problems. The person will try to change his or her action. However, just because a person may change outwardly does not mean that his foundation has changed. There must be a change in the heart. When a person receives love from other people, he starts to change.

Doctor, We Will Repair the
Roof of Your House

The hearts of people open when they receive love. Love is a precious thing that causes people to sacrifice for others. That is what opens people's hearts, allows their hearts to flow with one another, and makes them happy. In the same way that gold and silver are both elements but are different from one another, every person has a different personality. Some people have infinite hearts of love, while others harbor hatred and malice. Although they may all be people, but based on what they hold in their hearts, there is great differences between the hearts of the people of the world.

When I was about eight years old, my mother passed away. My father raised all five of us. At the time, my younger brother was suffering from a middle ear infection. These days, middle ear infections are easily treatable. Back then, however, there was not much medication, so it did not heal very well. My younger brother often had sweltering fevers in the middle of the night, and we would often have to take him to the hospital.

In the Seonsan countryside where I grew up, there was a small hospital called the Mingseng Hospital. That hospital was the only one in the area. The doctor at the hospital was a smart, high-level community leader in that region. Compared to him, my father was just a plain, uneducated farmer. When my father was alive, I did not notice it, but when I think of my father now, from time to time, I believe he was a very wise man although he was not well educated. Even after he passed away, I longed for my father. I missed him so much because I could so deeply feel the heart of my father who loved us so much. The love that my father bestowed upon us had no end.

Having said that, let me continue telling the story of my younger brother. He had a middle ear infection so my father asked his way around to find out where the doctor lived. At that time, most houses were made of straw, and his house was no exception. Straw houses had straw roofs. But after about a year, the straw would begin to rot. When this happened, the resident would have to thatch new straw and replace the roof. Although the doctor was good at healing diseases, he had never done that kind of work before. Upon seeing the doctor's house, my father quickly went to the hospital and told the doctor, "Doctor, I can see that the roof of your house needs to be replaced. I will come over one day and thatch your roof with new straw. Please remember this." After saying that one day, he carried over several bundles of straw and piled them up high in the doctor's yard. Then he began to thatch the straw. After thatching the straw for one day, two days, and three days, he took the thatched straw he made and tied them into bundles so that they would not blow away in the wind. He removed the old thatched straw from his roof and laid down the new straw.

Because his son had to go to the hospital often, my father needed to build a friendship with the doctor. If he were a person on the doctor's level, then he could have shared a drink with him. However, my father knew himself well, so he chose to do a job that was fitting to his level. He replaced the doctor's roof and rebuilt the doctor's walls when they started to collapse. At that time, bathrooms were outhouses, and my father knew when the doctor's outhouse would become full. When this happened, he would remove all the waste and cleaned the doctor's outhouse. Because of that, whenever my younger brother became sick in the middle of the night, he was able to take him to the doctor. Through this, a relationship of the heart was formed between the doctor and my father. They became really close. These kinds of things can only be accomplished by a father who truly loves his children.

The Heart of a Parent and the Heart of an Uncle Can never Be the Same

We have many people in our church, so we have many weddings. At our church we arrange marriages between men and women. If they love each other, we then provide a meeting between the parents of the man and the woman. The parents then get together and speak about the details of the wedding. They discuss things like when and where to hold the wedding. They also talk about where the newlyweds will start their new life together. If the parents of both the bride and the groom are present, then it is great. However, sometimes the mother or the father is missing. In such cases, the uncle or older brother comes in the place of the father to discuss the wedding. Everyone is grateful that the uncle or brother is taking the place of the father, but sometimes, uncles are not helpful at all. While discussing the wedding, there are times when the opinions of both sides do not fit. In such cases, the father does not try to exert his pride, or save face because he knows that his daughter will move into that family and start to live with them. Therefore, he does not speak from his personal feelings; he holds back by saying, "Sure, it would be great if we did that."

For example, if the parents of the groom live in Busan, and the parents of the bride live in Seoul, both parties would like to have the wedding where they live. This is because it would be easier for them to invite guests and it would be more convenient in every way. Therefore, one of the two parties must yield to the other. Their opinions are also different when deciding the wedding date because each family has their own circumstances to deal with. Both parties want the date that is most convenient for them. In such a situation, one or the other must yield. The interesting thing is that the mother and father who yield easily allow things to work out smoothly.

"If you do that, would you regret it?"

"No, not at all, Pastor. Isn't this what everyone does?"

They give in to one another so that the wedding preparation goes well. On the other hand, when it's the uncle or older brother, the discussions do not go so well. Because the mother and father came to discuss the wedding of their loving child, they do not push or force their own pride or try to save face. They do not worry about anything; they only have the heart to make things go well for their children.

On the other hand, the uncle or older brother is quite different. They give their money and time for the wedding of their nephew or younger brother, but they are unable to put everything else aside. If it seems their pride is being dashed, they show their displeasure and disappointment. At first, I did not know about this, but I now know that when an uncle or older brother shows up, the preparations for the wedding will not go smoothly. One does not become a mother or father by getting a license. It is also not done through studying a great amount or making a large sum of money. Carrying the baby in the womb for nine months, nurturing the baby, and risking her life to have that child is something only a mother can do. When a child is born, the breast milk for the child is automatically made. That is why there is no one who can take the place of the mother.

When I was young, I did not know my father's heart very well. But when my younger brother had his middle ear infection, my father did not think about his pride or his image; his only concern was gaining the doctor's heart at that time. He went and took charge of all the dirty jobs at the doctor's home. As I grew older, I began to feel just how much my father cared for immature kids like us. After having raised children of my own, when I think about the heart my father had, I am put to shame and I really miss him. I felt ashamed of all the days I did not obey him. In my heart I often feel, "If I could go back in time to my father, I would serve my father like this, and I would do that for him."

For the most part, young people cannot feel their parents' hearts very well. They only want to get what they desire from their fathers. It is for this reason that the loving heart of the father does not flow to them. That is why many young people live spewing nothing but complaints and bitterness.

The Minister Who Left His Son in the Hands of a Gangster

A long time ago in a certain nation, there was a well-admired minister. This minister was always lonely because he had no children. But late in his life, his wife conceived. This became known throughout the palace, and the king prepared a special herbal medicine for the minister's wife. Amidst many difficulties, the minister's old wife gave birth to a child, a son. The minister was overflowing with so much joy that he did not know what to do. However, as the child grew, it seemed like the child was missing something. Whenever he went out, the other children would always pick on him, and he would come home crying and beaten up. When he turned seventeen years old, it was time for him to get married. But he was still very immature. The minister thought deeply about this, and one day, he summoned a famous gangster. This gangster specialized in doing evil things. The gangster thought that he was going to die because the minister had summoned him. On the contrary, the minister set an elaborate spread on a table and told him to eat. The gangster felt so odd that he was unable to eat.

"Eat!" ordered the minister.

"Your humble servant is overwhelmed."

"I called you here because I have a special favor to ask of you."

"Your majesty, how could a person like me be of any service to you? But if you ask anything of me, I will put my life on the line to do it."

"Very well. I have a son, but even though he has come of age, he has not seen the country. Before I grow any older, I want to show my son each corner of our nation. I will pay for all travel expenses, so I want you to take my son and show him all the corners of the nation." The gangster was so happy to hear this. He replied, "I will do as you have commanded."

Immediately, the minister brought out a horse and put his son on it. He placed the reins in the gangster's hands and sent them on their journey. The minister's son was on the horse and the gangster was walking. But after walking for a while, the gangster's legs ached, and he began to patronize the minister's son.

"Sir, your legs look so strong," said the gangster.

"Yes, my legs are strong."

"My legs are so weak."

"Really? Then let me take the reins. Why don't you ride on the horse?"

"Would that be okay with you?"

"Sure, my legs are strong."

Now it was the gangster who was riding on the horse and the minister's son who was walking, all because the compliments the gangster paid to the minister's son made him feel good. With that, he held onto the reins and walked alongside the horse. But after walking for about ten or twenty miles, the son's legs began to hurt so much that he wanted to ride the horse. "Now I will ride the horse," said the minister's son.

"Sir, you are so healthy and strong, I'm sure your legs would not hurt even if you were to walk 100 miles." And so, even though the minister's son wanted to ride the horse, when he heard the gangster's words, he felt good and was uplifted again.

"You're right. My legs won't hurt."

Once again, the gangster manipulated the minister's son by continuing to flatter and make him feel good. However, his legs continued to ache and he became angry. "Hey, my legs are strong, but I've been walking a long way. Now I want to ride the horse."

"But sir, you are so healthy."

"But I'm still going to ride."

"Sir, my body is so weak."

"No! I'm going to ride."

Because the minister's son's legs ached terribly, he fought with the gangster. In this way the minister's son began to get the gangster under his control, little by little. "You are still trying to figure out how to manipulate me and use me, aren't you?" That is the way they toured the entire nation.

Then it became time to return home. The minister's son had become very smart.

"You gangster, you treated me like a fool, didn't you? Now that we are home, I am going to tell my father everything. Do you know what's going to happen to you?"

Now the gangster did not know what to do, and said, "I'm sorry, sir. I'm so sorry. I beg for your forgiveness."

After they completed their journey, they arrived at the minister's home.

"Father, we have returned."

"Well done. Did you have fun?"

"Yes, Father. But there is something I want to tell you, Father."

"What is it?"

"Father, why are you so bad at selecting people? Of all the people you could have chosen, why did you send a person like him with me? I feel sorry for the king who has to work with you."

When the minister heard this, he felt infinitely happy inside. When his son departed on the journey, he was not able to say such a thing. He was just a clumsy fool, but now he had returned with intelligence. As the minister listened to what his son had to say, his eyes began to fill with tears. "My son has wisdom and ability, but because I was so overprotective, he never learned how to use them."

At that moment, the minister said to his son, "You are right, and I was wrong."

Afterwards, the son became even wiser by the day. He followed in his father's footsteps and became a great king. Going through difficulties is absolutely necessary for a child to become strong and wise during the growth process. Even though the father knows that the son will suffer if he goes on the trip with the gangster, the father chooses to do so, because through that difficulty, his son can change. That is the father's heart. Young children need to know *this* heart of a father.

Once the Son Felt the Love of the Father, Change Happened in His Life

In the story of the rich father and his son mentioned in chapter 1, the younger son who left the house dreaming of greatness, ultimately returned home as a beggar. Right then, the father who had been waiting outside saw a beggar walking from a distance. He could see from the beggar's steps that it was his son. The father ran and fell on his son's neck and kissed him. Immediately, the son said to his father, "Father, I have sinned before heaven and you. Now I am no more worthy to be called thy son." However, regardless of what his son was saying, the father spoke to the servants and said, "Bring forth the best robe and put it on him. Put a ring on his hand, and shoes on his feet." This expresses the heart of the father extremely well.

People have eyes, a nose, a mouth, and ears. But above all else, people have hearts: the heart to love their children and the heart to sacrifice for their children. This is something only the mother and father can have, and is something that no one can duplicate. Parents want their children to be well. They want their children to grow to become someone great.

The problem with many young people is that their hearts are blocked from their fathers. When children converse with their fathers from their hearts, and listen to their fathers' words, they can tell that within their fathers' hearts is the love that wants their children to be well. Even though at times, a father becomes angry and scolds his son. When he listens closely to the words of his father, he can feel his father's heart of love. When children feel their father's love, then change begins to happen in their lives. Students who used to live crooked lives are able to hold their hearts the right way once they come to know their father's heart. "I've been wrong. I shouldn't be acting this way." Because of this, fathers should pour their love upon their children and not expect their children to change overnight. They should pour their hearts onto their children, little by little.

If the parents love and sacrifice for their children, then the children, who once only cared about themselves, will finally begin to feel that love, and they will be touched. When the parents' hearts, which are full of love, flow into their children, then the young people who have fallen victim to gaming, drinking, gambling, and living riotously, can overcome the desires inside them. Their mother and father have a heart that is for their children. Beautiful mothers have such a heart, and even mothers who are not beautiful have such a heart. Educated mothers have the heart to love their children, and uneducated mothers also have the same heart to love their children. Mothers with lots of money take care of their children with the money they have. And mothers without money care for and love their children without money.

When the children feel the parents' hearts of love and sacrifice, it will change their hearts.

When children think about how their father always nags at them and yells at them, they start to complain. But when they feel the love their father has in his heart, that sincerely wants them to do well, that is when they begin, little by little, to open their hearts to their parents. When their hearts are open to their parents, then the hearts of the children and the parents flow into one another. They will then be able to speak about what is in their hearts to their fathers and listen to what is in their fathers' hearts. When their hearts flow together in this manner, the parents' and children's hearts become one. Then when their hearts become one, it is very easy to fix the bad ways of life.

On the other hand, when people remain isolated, it is very difficult to fix their wrongful way of life. Whether quitting alcohol, drugs, gambling, or computer games, it is very difficult. And even though the children do not want to do these things, the heart of wanting to do them continually arises. But even though the children are in such a state, if they realize their father's heart and his love for them, then the father's heart begins to flow in them. And when that happens, changing their hearts is easily accomplished.

People Chase after the Things They See with Their Eyes because They Have not Seen Anything Better

A long time ago, before I founded the International Youth Fellowship, I visited Los Angeles, where I met a young man. One day, his mother, whom I knew, came to see me. She said, "Pastor, please help my son, Andy. I worry about him and it makes me cry every single day."

I listened to what his mother said, and replied, "I live in Korea and your son lives in America, so how can I help him?" It really seemed as if there was no way I could help him. Nevertheless, she came to talk to me three times because of her son.

Later on, she choked up as she was talking, "My son does drugs, and these days, he is carrying around a gun. I know something is going to happen. I'm so scared, and there is nothing I can do."

This woman was living with her son after she got divorced. She studied hard without her husband and passed the CPA exam. She was quite wealthy, and because they were financially well off, she could do everything for her only son. She bought him the most expensive clothing. Even with fruit, she only bought the biggest and best for him. She bought him the best food. Whatever she bought for him, she only bought the best. She wanted other people to say that she had raised her son well. She sent her son to the best school and had him study there. But when Andy turned 14 years old, he started using drugs.

Then one day, she saw a gun in her son's pocket and was completely shocked.

"Andy, why are you acting like this? You are my everything. Please, stop acting like this."

"Mom, I'm not living like this because I want to. I want to live the right way, but I can't. You know, I just want to die because I'm like this. It's terrible enough as it is. Mom, I don't need you to jump on me even more. Just leave me alone!"

From that day on, the conversation between Andy and his mother ended. Actually, Andy wanted to be good to his mother, because he knew that his mother sacrificed everything for him. He wanted to make her happy, but whenever he got together with his friends, he would do drugs and fall victim to terrible things. She cried and sincerely asked me to take care of her son and help him. "Would it be okay for me to take Andy to Korea?" I asked.

"Sure, please take him," Andy's mother replied.

I brought her son to Korea. I had never seen a child who lived the way he did—the way he dressed, and the way he acted. He did things that I had never seen or heard before in my life. He had these torn-up, baggy pants that barely hung onto his butt. I would say to him, "Andy, your pants are falling off." He also had a weird haircut with rainbow colors. The reason why he wore his pants like that and acted that way was because that was what looked good to him. So, instead of rebuking him, I wanted to show him something better. From time to time I spoke to Andy about the world of the heart. I primarily explained the things in the Bible to him.

One day he completely changed. As he came to know the world of the heart, he opened his heart and accepted the hearts of others. Afterwards, he dressed nicely and neatly, and he got a nice, clean haircut. Andy is very handsome when he smiles. He has such a beautiful face. I felt it was such a loss that he had lived with a frown on his face all this time. One day, Andy's father came to see his son because he heard his son was in Korea. This was the first time he had seen him in years. Andy explained to his father how he had changed.

"Father, are you happy?" Andy asked.

"I'm very happy."

"Father, if you read the Bible, you, too, will become happy. Father, I want you to be happy."

He began to cry at his son's words and said to me, "Pastor, my son has really changed. Thank you!"

Currently, Andy is an English teacher at the Gracias Music Preparatory School in Daejeon. Again, he is living a completely new life.

What Will Moving the Hand on the Gauge to the Top Do When You Are out of Fuel?

Everyone makes mistakes. There is not a single person who does everything right. Young people do not have much experience, so when something looks good to them, they run toward it and easily fall into it. Whether it's drugs, gambling, video games, or alcohol, they fall into these kinds of things very easily. And once they do fall into these things, later on, they try to break free, but it does not work because their hearts have already been soaked into them, and they have started to enjoy those things. However, if they realize the condition of their hearts, and as their hearts connect with others, they can easily break out and be free from everything.

When a car runs out of fuel, the hand on the fuel gauge points to the bottom. When we see this, we go to the gas station and put in fuel. Then the hand on the gauge goes back up again. But while we're driving, if we see that the fuel gauge hand is pointing to the bottom, and ask, "Why is the hand pointing to the bottom?" then we break the glass on the gauge and force the needle to face upward, will that work? It is the fuel that has to goes into the tank that makes the needle go up again. Just because you bend the hands to point upwards, it does not solve anything.

This is also true with people's hearts. When there is no love in people's hearts, and when there is no exchange with other people and they live isolated, people try to solve their problems on their own. However, genuine change does not happen through outward changes. There has to be a change at the core of the heart. That is the force that changes our actions. Therefore, when your heart flows with other people, and when their peace and their joy enter you and remain there, that is when your life begins to change.

Through the World Camp, I was able to see many college students who had lived with darkness and problems change their lives up close. They were able to have that change because a new heart entered them. No matter whom it is, their lives change when they open their hearts. That is why no one is as foolish as the person who has his or her heart closed.

"I'm right, so I don't want to listen to you."

"I don't need to listen to you. You are wrong."

There is no one with as serious a problem as the person who says this. The mentally ill never listen to others. People who are always busy thinking that they are right and exerting their own opinions and stubbornness are bound to end up in mental hospitals. We need to learn how to think deeply. We have to think about the kind of people that we are and open our hearts to listen to what other people say. We have to learn to listen closely. Then, when our hearts flow into one another, our lives become healthy and beautiful.

Chapter 8

Discovery

New Life Begins When You Become Connected to a Different Heart.

According to what you accept into your heart, there will be a difference in life. If you accept a bright and clean heart, then you will live a bright and clean life. In order for this to happen, you must lower your heart, then a much happier life can come.

People Who Give Themselves a Generous Score Have Lives that Become Tiring and Filled with Problems

If people who do not know themselves very well were told to rate themselves, they would rate themselves much higher than if someone else were to rate them.

In reality there are many people who have been rated a fifty by other people, but have rated themselves over eighty. People like this often clash with the people around them because they see themselves as an eighty, while others see them and treat them as a fifty. One person might think to himself, "Why are these people despising me?" and a conflict starts. On the other hand, if a person has been rated a fifty but only rates himself a thirty, then that person would always have a thankful heart towards those around him. And because people treat him and see him as a fifty, he would end up having good relationships with people.

This is also true between a husband and a wife. "My husband is so great; I'm so lucky that this man married a woman like me." A woman with this heart will feel, "Since my husband is better than I am in every way, if I tell him about my problem, he will take care of it," whenever she has a difficulty. She then tells her husband her problems and begins to rest. She is able to have peace because it is now her husband who takes on the task. On the other hand, a woman who thinks, "I am much better than my husband. My husband is good for nothing," cannot give her problems to her husband and whenever she has problems; she holds onto everything herself. She eventually ends up nagging and complaining about her husband. As she does this, she places the blame on her husband when things go wrong, and she hides her own weak image.

If you humble your heart and position it a little lower than where it really is, you will be able to communicate very well with the people around you. As a result, you will start to become happy. But, if you judge yourself to be better than you actually are, then everything appears worthy of complaint. For example, if a person who makes sixty thousand dollars a year thinks like a person who makes thirty thousand dollars a year, then he would be very frugal with the way he spends his money. He would be completely satisfied with whatever clothes he buys, and the food that he eats would be delicious. On the other hand, if a person who makes sixty thousand dollars a year lives like a person who makes one hundred thousand dollars a year, then no matter what he buys, he is full of complaints. Because the bar is set high, his pockets cannot keep up. Therefore, even though people may not be able to live in a plentiful environment, if they discipline their hearts well, they can be happy even though they are poor. In order for that to occur, the most important thing is to discover one's self. Sadly, ninety-nine percent of people score themselves higher than they actually are.

The Metal Wire around the Monkey's Neck that It Cannot Undo on Its Own

There is a story about a monkey by a man named, Andrew, who was a soldier from the Netherlands that was deployed to Indonesia. When he got there, he bought a monkey from the locals and was raising it in the army barracks. Andrew saw many of his colleagues die during different battles, and as he killed many enemy soldiers, his mind became very sharp, sensitive, and tormented. After a battle he would always go into the forest with his pet monkey, and they would take walks together. This had been a source of comfort for Andrew. The monkey followed Andrew around well enough, and the two of them got along very well.

But after a while, the monkey lost its appetite and became very depressed. Andrew did not understand why. One day, Andrew took his monkey and went into the woods in order to escape from the memories and terror of battle. As he lay on the grass and looked up at the sky, petting the monkey that was sitting on his chest, he felt something around the monkey's neck. When he took a closer look, it was a metal wire. When the monkey was very little, someone had placed a metal wire around its neck. As the monkey grew, however, its neck became thicker and now the wire was starting to choke him. The wire was underneath the fur so it had not been visible. However, that day, by chance, Andrew was able to feel the wire that was wrapped around the monkey's neck.

Andrew made up his mind to cut the wire. He took a very sharp knife and a pair of pliers, and when he went into the woods, he explained everything to the monkey. "You're in pain because this wire is wrapped around your neck. I'll cut this off for you." The monkey stood still as if he understood. With his right leg Andrew held down the monkey's body and found the knot of metal wire that was wrapped around its neck. With his knife, Andrew removed the skin that was covering the knot of wire. The monkey was bleeding, but handled everything quite well. After he pulled out the knot, he cut one end, and held the other with a pair of pliers. He then proceeded to pull out the wire from the opposite side, which completely released the monkey's neck. The monkey bled, but as the wound healed, the monkey was back to its energetic ways.

Even though a metal wire is nothing to a human being, a monkey can never untie a wire on its own. A person can easily cut the knot and remove the metal wire, but it is impossible for a monkey to do it. In the same way that the monkey was unable to untie the metal wire wrapped around its neck, even though a person may be smart or well-educated, there are problems that he cannot solve on his own. At that moment, if there is a person present who is able to help with the problems, then he can easily be freed from his problems, just as Andrew freed the monkey from its pain.

If only I Could Straighten Out His Hand, which Has Folded like a Mitten

The International Youth Fellowship trains college students who participated in the World Camp to become future leaders who will lead the world. We may not know right now, but among these students, there could be a future Secretary General of the UN, a minister, or even the president of a country.

When we study history, we learn about the history of wars. Wars are fought by soldiers, but the soldiers do not have the power to make the decisions about waging them. A war is waged through the decision of just a few politicians. The president, king, or other leaders decide on waging the war, but they do not go into battle themselves. Among the chronicles of the kings of Israel, there were kings who often caused wars because of their aggressive personalities. Because of them, many soldiers shed their blood. We can also see heart wrenching scenes of innocent people being killed, and many children becoming orphans, throughout the history of war. When the young people who graduate from the International Youth Fellowship become politicians and presidents, they will not cause tragedies like war as a result of their aggressive personalities. Even now, we have prepared programs that will soften the hearts of the students. To soften the heart, you need security. In order to gain the security of the heart, both spiritual life and music are very effective. We always invite the world's greatest musicians to allow students to hear the world's best music. We have also formed the Gracias Choir. Not only do they sing, but they also express their hearts through music.

Among the choir members, there is a person named Douglas, who is from Ghana. Douglas has a brilliant bass voice. It is a little rough, but quite smooth all at the same time. He has a voice that embodies the unique sound of Africa. The timbre of his voice itself is good, but the true value of his voice comes out most when it harmonizes with the other voices of the choir. When Douglas embraces the song with his low tone, all the other mistakes and ranges are covered up, and it softens the music. We notice a difference in the choir when Douglas is not there. Unfortunately, Douglas's right hand is disfigured into the shape of a fist. I asked him why his hand was that way, and he said that it was because he had been burned. If he had been able to straighten his hand out when he burned his arm at a young age, then he would have been able to move all of his fingers. Because his hand was neglected in its burned state, all his fingers became fused to one another, and he had lived that way for twenty-three years. When I held Douglas's hand and looked closely at it, I noticed that all of his fingers were there. So I took Douglas to Hanyang University Hospital and had a discussion with him and a plastic surgeon. We discussed performing surgery on his fingers. The doctor said, "Let's try it," and we agreed. I was so happy thinking about the fact that Douglas's hand would be straightened out, and that it would finally be a normal hand. We went to the hospital a few more times. There was one time when he asked for the opinion of the orthopedic surgeon. The orthopedic surgeon looked and said that the surgery was not going to work. "We can separate the fingers which were fused together. But even if you did separate these fingers, which had been bent for twenty-three years, they would never straighten out. Physical therapy would not change that." Although Douglas looked forward to living with a normal hand, we had no choice but to leave the hospital. Had his hand been straightened out immediately after he was burned, he would have been able to use his hand like a normal person. But Douglas's parents did not know this, and in Africa, because medical care is so expensive, he did not dare go to the hospital. Therefore, his precious hand was left the way it was and it ended up becoming stiff. In Africa, Douglas is not the only one with a hand like this; in fact, there are many people who do not have an arm or a leg. When bitten by bugs, attacked by animals, or wounded, people have to take extreme measures such as amputation because they were not treated immediately.

The Change of a College Student Who Had Been Addicted to Computer Games

When I look at many college students, they remind me of Douglas. This is because the world of their hearts is like Douglas's hand. Students who have been led the correct way from early on in their lives are fine. But those whose hearts were neglected often face very serious situations later on in life. Since college students have pure hearts, they do not have many fixed thoughts. They are quick to understand things and are good at receiving the hearts of others. That is why they change so easily. Whenever I give my "Mind Lectures," the students accept what they have heard and experience great change in their lives.

In actuality the problems that college students face tend to be game addiction, gambling, sex corruption, problems with friends, inferiority complexes, or bitterness towards their divorced parents. Although they appear to be complicated, when you get closer to them, you can see they are actually quite simple. Like when you open the hood of a car, it looks very complicated, but it's actually quite simple once you know the parts. There are 30,000 parts in a car: the power system, the braking system, the electrical system, the cooling system, the steering system, etc. But when you divide them up according to their functions, it becomes very simple. It only appears complicated when you mix them all together. For example, when you open up a TV or a computer, everything looks extremely complicated. But when you understand just a few systems, it all becomes very simple. In the same way, while it seems that college students have a huge, diverse range of problems, when you divide the world of their hearts into several parts and then look at them, it all becomes quite simple as well. When you give them just a little bit of guidance, the conditions of their hearts greatly improve.

A student from Ehwa Women's University attended the World Camp. She was very beautiful and she was a very smart student. Unfortunately, she had fallen into video game addiction. She said that she once played 37 hours of video games without rest. She would order Jajang noodles, and eat them while playing. In the beginning, she played video games just for fun, but then she began to fall into them more and more. She would eat breakfast, leave her home for school, but then she would end up going to the Internet cafés. She would tell herself, "I should go to school," and she would actually get on the bus to go to school. Soon afterwards she would get off the bus and head to the Internet café.

Her parents had no idea that their daughter was this way. When she had finally reached the point where she could no longer study, she attended the World Camp. If you are a college student, before anyone even says anything, you can recognize that you have become a video game addict. When you realize that this is keeping you from studying, you try to quit playing the games. Nevertheless, when your parents tell you to stop, because you have already tried to quit before they reprimanded you, you feel even more burdened. Most importantly, even though you try not to play video games on your own, you cannot stop. That is when your father continues to scold you. As a result, you end up having a heart full of frustration and rebellion.

I had no idea that this student had fallen into video game addiction, and so the World Camp simply ran according to its schedule. This student attended the World Camp, listened to great music, talked with students from different countries, and shared her heart with the friends in her class. As she spent each day like this, her heart automatically changed, and at one point, she was completely free from her game addiction.

In the story of the prodigal son, he also must have thought many times that he needed to break free from the prostitute's house. At a glance, it seems that he could just walk out on his own two feet, but when a person falls into a place like this, that is the thing that becomes the most difficult for him to do. That is why it means absolutely nothing to tell students who have fallen into gaming or sex addiction not to do those things. This is because they have already tried very hard to quit themselves, but it did not work. All it does is add extra burden and conflict in their hearts. Quite frankly, it does not help them break free from their addiction in any way. Students who have this kind of isolated world of the heart must be moved in a different direction. A different thought must enter into their hearts. When a different thought enters them, people begin to change. It is for this reason that we must open their hearts so that we can accept a thought that is different from our own because the more fixated we are on quitting, the deeper we fall into our addictions. We must lead their hearts to a place where they can depart from these things

Think about this situation. Suppose a male student were having a relationship with a female student but met the opposition of his parents. As a result, the father does not allow his son to go outside and makes him study only in his room. The father occasionally enters his son's room and says, "Hey! You're thinking about her again, aren't you? What's so great about her? If you see her again, you are going to ruin your life." If he does this, then his son, who was trying to grab a hold of his own heart, ends up becoming even more fixated on the girl. How could he forget her now? The more his father stresses that this female student is a bad person, the more his son will think about her and want to spend time with her. From the son's point of view, his father's attempts to belittle her does not stop him from thinking about her, but rather provokes him to think about her even more. Therefore, in order for his son to stop thinking about her, the father must lead his son's heart into in a totally different direction.

What Kind of Couple Divides the Wife's and Husband's Possessions?

There is a missionary I am quite close to. His wife used to work at a bank, and she was very good at what she did. When she was a bank teller, she was so quick that although there were long lines at other windows, the customers at her window would go through very quickly. In a short time, there would be no line at her window. She lived being constantly recognized at her bank, but after getting married, she left the bank and followed her husband to Africa. This lady did not really care much about spiritual life, but through her husband, she became the wife of a missionary. In Africa, there were very few privileges of civilization, so there were lots of discomforts. It was very painful for this missionary's wife to live there.

"The people here even smell different. Look at all these insects! I really hate this weather. Why is there no running water?" She was always full of complaints. She actually tried to endure everything, but she could not bear it any longer and thought of returning to Korea. She even determined in her heart to do just that.

One evening her husband came to her with an excited face and said, "Honey! They told us to go into the jungle to teach the people there about the Bible for two weeks. I am so thankful! Aren't you?"

"Thankful? I am not thankful at all!" she thought. Those words came to the tip of her tongue, but because she saw how deeply touched her husband was, it was hard for her to throw this at him. Her husband continued to speak,

"Honey, even though we don't know the language and there are many other people who do speak the language better than we can, it is such a special grace that we have been chosen to go! We get to meet and preach the Gospel to the people in the jungle! Aren't you thankful?" Seeing the sincere expression on her husband's face, she unknowingly answered, "Yes, I am thankful." It was difficult enough living in the city, but now she had no choice but to follow her husband and travel all the way into the jungle.

The couple was living in Tema, which is a city in Ghana. They took a four-hour bus ride from there to the city of Kumasi. Then from Kumasi there was no bus, so they had to hitch a ride on a logging truck and ride on the rugged road for several hours. From there, there were no roads at all, and no vehicles could go any further. However, there was a person waiting to guide them the rest of the way. They followed their guide into the jungle. And because the jungles are thicker than forests, it is dark even during the day. And since there are so many trees, you cannot walk standing upright. The person in the front had a huge machete, and struck away at the trees and bushes to carve out a path to travel on.

They walked this way into the jungle for several hours and finally arrived at the local village. It was a village that was settled deep into the jungle, so there were forty to fifty huts there. They had to cut down many trees and these huts were made with banana and coconut leaves that were bonded together. In the yards, chickens ran around and there were also a few dogs and monkeys playing around as well. It was the first time a "white man" was visiting this village. We divide people into many different races, but in Africa, people tend to divide people into two categories: white and black. That is why even Koreans are considered white if they go to Africa. Everyone in the village gathered to see the missionary and his wife. They touched the missionary's hands, then his face, and were so amazed to see people that looked like them.

Because there was no clock in the village, it was meaningless to say, "Let's meet up at this time." There was no set time to hold a service, but when there was a nice gathering of people, the missionary would speak to them about the Bible. Even as they listened, there were people who were whispering to one another, people who were lying down, people who were just sitting there, and lots of other people f people doing different things. Even still the missionary and his wife began to speak with the people, little by little, with their broken language. That was how they spent their time there.

One day a couple came to them with two eggs and told them to eat them. They were so thankful. One person brought them bananas, another person brought them papayas, other people brought them coconuts, someone brought them some mangos, and some people killed and brought them a chicken, which was considered very precious there. A few days later, the man who had actually invited the missionary and his wife to the village spoke to them. "Missionary, I am very sorry."

"About what?"

"Although I have invited you here, I have nothing to give you. All the chickens in this yard belong to my wife. Out of the banana and coconut trees here, mine are the ones with no fruit remaining. All the trees full of fruit are my wife's trees. Although my wife is rich, I am poor."

The people in this village marry easily, but they also get divorced quite easily. Therefore, even though a man and a woman are married and become a couple, they think about what might happen later on, so they do not share their wealth. They are very clear about which possessions belong to them, so you are not able to touch anything unless it is yours. That was how it was in the jungle, a place where you are considered rich, even if you only have two pots and two sets of clothes."

When the missionary's wife heard this man speak about this life, it was strange to her. Even if you added up all the bananas, coconuts, and chickens they owned together, it would only come out to about fifty dollars or so. It seemed so childish to divide it up. "This belongs to the wife, and this belongs to the husband." It was so childish to her that she could not understand it. She thought to herself, "If I were her, I'd say, 'Honey, are you hungry? You can have my bananas.' If she were to do that, how happy and joyful would her husband be? How could they even call themselves a couple when they divide up everything they own into hers and his?"

As she thought more about this, the missionary's wife became shocked. Because although she was not acting this way toward her husband with bananas, but with other things, she was clearly dividing up what belonged to her husband and what was her own. Ultimately, she discovered that she was no different from the people in the village. At first, she thought that they were wrong, but she realized that she, too, was wrong. And on top of all of that, while the people in the jungle were satisfied with having just one pot, she desired so many things. "I was greedy for many vain things instead of wanting to be together with my husband. I had lost my heart to superficial things!" From then on, the missionary's wife's heart changed and her life also completely changed. When people have their eyes opened to clearly see their image, they change. People who live following after the ambitions that arise in them everyday cannot change. On the other hand, the people who realize, "This was terribly wrong. I should have done it this way. Why did I act that way?" after doing something wrong, are those who can be changed and become new.

When the Time Comes, a Caterpillar Changes into a Beautiful Butterfly without any Cosmetic Surgery

A few years ago, I met a drug addict in America named Tommy. After my sermon he came to me and said, "Tonight, your words touched my heart greatly." Then he told me about the life he had lived.

"I met a Korean woman in America. This woman did not have a green card, but I knew that if she lived with me, she could get her citizenship. So she married me even though I was a drug addict. My wife is as beautiful as an angel, and she would work so hard to make money. But I am the devil that takes her money and spends it all on drugs."

So I asked Tommy, "Tommy, have you ever seen a butterfly?"

"Sure, there are not many in L.A., but I do see them from time to time."

"Do you think butterflies are beautiful?"

"Yes, I think they are beautiful."

"Tommy, do you know which bug becomes a butterfly? You may think that because butterflies look beautiful, that a beautiful bug becomes a butterfly. But, that is not the case. Actually, the bug that becomes a butterfly is initially a pretty disgusting bug. Isn't that correct?"

"Are you saying that I am going to become a butterfly?"

"Suppose you could have a conversation with that disgusting bug. What would you say to it? 'Hey bug, don't despair. You are a disgusting looking insect now, but in just a little while; you will shed that body of yours and turn into a beautiful butterfly.' Isn't that what you would say? Then, what would the bug say to you? 'Me? I will one day become a butterfly? Don't make me laugh. I look this disgusting. How could I ever become a butterfly? I am just a caterpillar. I am just going to simply eat cabbage leaves until I die. Look at how beautiful that butterfly is. I cannot become a butterfly.' That is what it would say. Then, you will say, 'No, caterpillar, that butterfly was once a caterpillar a long time ago just like you are now. A caterpillar was made so that it could become a butterfly. When you look at your current state, it seems like you will continue to crawl around for the rest of your life and just die that way. However, the Lord, the Creator, has given you the ability to become a butterfly one day.' Tommy, I've met many murderers and death-row inmates in prison. I've met many drug addicts, alcoholics, and game addicts. The problem was that they all had fallen into themselves. But there was not a single person that did not change when they opened their hearts and shared what was in their hearts in words. Right now, your thoughts and my thoughts are different, but when we keep talking with one another, my thoughts will enter your heart and without you even knowing it, your heart will change to be like mine. And when you get closer and closer to my heart, you can throw away your wrongful life. That is why it is very important to open your heart and speak."

"Pastor, even if I have conversations, people like me will not change."

"Tommy, you have no idea. The city that you live in now, do you think it was this nice of a city filled with trees to begin with? The Rocky Mountains to the east block out the clouds and there is almost no rain in L.A. all year long. You know that, right? That's why, a long time ago, this place was not a city but a desert. It was a complete desert where not a single tree or a single blade of grass could grow. Do you know how L.A. became such a beautiful city?

"People saw that this location was geographically fit to be a harbor and that the climate was good. Therefore, they brought water here from the Colorado River. They used very large pipes to draw the water from the river, and with smaller pipes they distributed water to all the parts of the city. That's how this city was formed. With that water, people wash and cook. They water the flowers and trees in their gardens and that's how they live. When it's morning in various parts of the city, sprinklers come out and water the plants causing flowers to bloom and trees to grow. This makes L.A. one of the best cities to live in the world. When the river water is brought in, then the desert is no longer a desert. It becomes a city where flowers bloom, trees grow, and the birds sing. This makes people like L.A. and has caused many people from all over the world to move to L.A. in order to build houses, set up schools, and run businesses. That is how it became such a big city.

If you block off the pipes that are connected to the Colorado River, the people in L.A. could not continue to live here for even one week. But just as the river water came in and changed this dried desert into a beautiful city overflowing with tourism, culture, education and life, it is the same with people's hearts. Tommy, you are this way because your heart has hardened and you are depressed, but do not be worried or afraid. If you receive a new thought and if you accept a new world into your heart, then just as this desert that had nothing but death, received water from the Colorado River, transforming it into L.A., your heart can also become new."

That day, Tommy changed his heart. He finally ended his life of being a drug addict, and he began to lead a new life.

Are you doing drugs or falling into bad habits? Do not strain yourself to quit drugs on your own, or try to fix your bad habits yourself. Accept the good heart that other people have. That heart will lead you, and you can become free as it leads you to depart from drugs, gambling, and or other bad behavior. When you try to change your life on your own, it is extremely difficult. You eventually end up giving up along the way. Then after failing several times, you end up becoming a person who lives having completely fallen into that. No matter who you are, everybody has a heart, and depending on what you accept into that heart, your way of life will differ. When you accept a bright and healthy heart, you come to live a bright and healthy life. But in order to accept such a heart, you must first humble your heart. When you live humbling yourself to a level that is lower than where you actually think you are, a much happier life will await you.

Chapter 9

Happiness

Happiness Is to Live Feeling the Flavor of a Person

You must live feeling another's flavor to be happy. Just as fruits have different flavors, people too have different flavors. No matter who they are, if you treat them with your heart, you get to feel their flavor and once you feel their flavor, you get to understand his or her random actions. Then, the same heart flows and the love inside the heart makes happiness.

Father, It's All Over for Us

A father and his son were traveling through a desert and lost their way. As they were lost, struggling this way and that way, they ran out of food and water. The two of them were walking through the desert and the son became exhausted; however, the older father was continuing to walk steadfast. It was because the father had hope, but the son did not.

When you buy a car, even though all the cars may appear to be the same on the outside, there is a great difference in price depending on the options. Cars with next to no options are cheap. Nowadays, technology is very advanced, so new options are continually being featured. You can add on a better braking system to a car. You can install better heaters and air conditioners. As you add on many kinds of cutting edge functions, there is a greater price difference between these cars and the ones that are only good at going back and forth. Riding in a car that has many options is both very nice and convenient. Even though it may be the same type of car, depending on the engine, there is a difference in power. In addition, depending on what brakes are installed, the car's ability to brake also differs. The better car has many options so that it will not slide in the snow and it will be safer in the rain. You cannot tell by just looking at the outside of the car, but when you actually drive the car, you feel a noticeable difference.

There are options for people's hearts as well. Because people's hearts are always changing, you cannot say that every heart is the same. Nevertheless, with people who have love in their hearts, that love impacts their lives. It is the same with people who have hope, and it is the same with people who have joy. On the other hand, people who are filled with hatred in their hearts, and people who are filled with complaints in their hearts, are also influenced by these things. Outwardly, they are the same humans, but people who have negative hearts are not happy in their lives.

A father and son were both lost in the desert, and they were both exhausted, but the father was completely different from his son. What kind of words would come from the lips of the son, who was only filled with despair? Would they be words of joy? Would they be words of thankfulness?

Naturally, the son only spoke negative words. "Father, we are going to die. Father, I cannot walk anymore. We're going to die anyway, so what's the point of walking?"

Why does he speak this way? It is because he has nothing but despair inside of him.

The father, on the other hand, says things that are completely different. "Son, we will not die. Why would we die?"

"Father, we are out of water. How can we not die? We are eventually going to die!"

"No, we are not. I've been through this desert many times, and I know this desert very well. Yes, we are lost. As you know, the paths in the desert are always changing because of sandstorms. But I have gotten lost many times. Each time that it has happened, do you know what I did? I walked towards the east. You saw the sunrise today, didn't you? Right now we are walking east. If you continue to walk just a little further, then you'll reach the end of the desert."

"Father, you are lying, aren't you? You are trying to deceive me. Where is the end of the desert? We walked all day yesterday, and there is no end in sight."

"You're right, we have not reached the end of the desert, yet. But we are getting very close. We'll be there either late today or by tomorrow, so be strong and let's continue to walk!" The father stirred up his son's heart in order to make him walk again. North, south, east, and west all displayed nothing but sand.

They were continuing to walk through the desert when the son screamed, out, "Father, look over there!"

The son was pointing to a tomb. Once the father and son drew closer to the tomb, the son fell to the ground and sat there. "Father, now it's surely over for us. Look at this tomb. Surely this person must have also gotten lost and struggled to survive, and then he must have died of thirst just like we are about to. We are going to die, aren't we? If we die, how are we going to let mother know that we've died? If we die, how will my little brothers live? Father, why did you get lost? Father!"

The son sat there in despair, but then the father said to him, "Son, now we've made it."

"We've made it? How can we survive in the middle of the desert?"

"Suppose this person in the tomb was lost and died of thirst like you said. Do you think he dug his own grave and climbed in? That couldn't happen. This means that there must have been someone else who buried this dead man. We do not see the other person's dead body here. That means that he or she did not die. Think about it. Graves are always close to a village where people live. The fact that there is a grave here is proof that we are near a village."

Although they were both looking at the same tomb, the son's thoughts and the father's thoughts were completely different. Even though they were standing in front of the same thing, the conclusions of people whose hearts are full of despair, and the conclusions of people with hope are on completely different levels. As we live our lives, the reasons that we complain and become bitter are not due to bad circumstances. It is the heart of darkness that creates complaints and bitterness in us. Joy and happiness are also not created by the circumstances, but by the hope and love in the heart.

Because the son's heart was full of despair, he was only filled with pain and suffering, but the father who had hope, was filled with joy. The father tried to relay the joy that was in his heart to his son, but his son did not receive his father's heart. "It's only natural for me to be full of despair right now." That was what the son thought, so there was no room for his father's hope to flow into him. If the son had received his father's heart from the beginning, then he could have received the strength to rejoice when his father rejoiced. But the son was unable to do so. He was busy exerting his own thoughts, and he was unable to receive the hope that was in his father. Although he walked on the same path as his father, he was being led into pain and suffering.

No matter how much knowledge or experience we have, it does not mean that we know everything. That is why, so often, when we listen to other people's words and accept that person's heart, we can receive the joy, happiness, and peace that we did not have. But for us to accept all the things we do not have into our hearts, we must lower the level of our hearts. We must acknowledge, "I really have many shortcomings. My heart is so weak, and I am a foolish person." Only a person who realizes this can accept what other people say, both when it fits their hearts and when it does not fit their hearts.

If You Don't Jump into the Sea, I'll Shoot You

A captain from Spain took his twelve-year-old son aboard his ship and sailed out to sea. Before, when the captain would go out to sea for months at a time, whenever he returned home, he saw that his son had grown so much that he could barely recognize him. The captain was always concerned that he didn't get to spend much time with his son. And so one day, the captain decided that he wanted to show the ocean to his growing son, so he decided to take his son with him on a voyage. Before the captain set sail, he told his son, "When we go out to sea, all you will see is the sky and ocean, so you will get very bored. Bring some toys and many books to read."

His son was filled with excitement about going on his first voyage to sea with his father. He packed his toys and books, and he brought his monkey, who was like a friend to him. Finally, the ship set sail, broke harbor and headed out toward the open sea. As the voyage started, the father, who was the captain, was very busy. He directed the sailors to work, and held meetings to discuss what they needed to do. The son soon became bored reading books and playing with his toys, so he started to play with his pet monkey. After having fun for a while, the monkey took the son's hat and ran away. He took his hat and ran throughout the entire ship with the hat. When the monkey had nowhere else to go, it started to climb up the main mast. The son wanted to recover his hat, so he quickly followed the monkey up the mast. As soon as he would go up one more level of the mast, the monkey would go up to another level. And then when the son would follow to the next level, the monkey went up another level. As they continued to do this, the monkey reached the top of the mast. The son also reached the top of the mast and thought, "Now I've got you." The moment he reached out his hand towards the monkey, the monkey hopped down and slid all the way down to the bottom of the mast.

Right then the son realized that he was at the very top of the mast. When the mast started to waver and the people on the deck appeared to be so small to him, he suddenly became very afraid. Having only concentrated on catching his monkey, he had followed it all the way to the top of the mast without even realizing what he was doing. After realizing the full extent of the situation, he was so afraid of falling that he became petrified. He held tightly onto the mast and began to shake and tremble. Because he was holding onto on to the mast with all his might, his arms started to grow weaker and weaker. It was then that one of the sailors saw the captain's son at the top of the mast. He cried out, "The captain's son is on at the top of the mast!" Then all of the sailors onboard gathered around the bottom. They were all worried, but there was no one who could go up to the top in time to save the captain's son. All they could do was look up and worry.

"What are we going to do about this? If he runs out of strength then he's going fall and will surely die." One of the sailors went to the captain's cabin and knocked on the door.

"Captain! Captain! We have a big problem!" The captain ran out onto the deck. "Look up there, sir!"

When he looked up, he saw his son clinging to the top of the mast and trembling in fear. "How did this happen?"

One of the sailors pointed towards the monkey who was holding the boy's hat and told him, "Your son was following the monkey to recover his hat, sir. That's what happened."

The captain thought to himself for a moment, and then he pulled out his pistol. The sailors were stunned and started to mumble among themselves. "What's the point of shooting the monkey now?" But then, all of a sudden the captain aimed his gun at his son and said, "Son, can you hear me?"

"Yes, Father."

"I want you to jump from the top of the mast into the ocean right now. Otherwise, I will shoot you with this gun." However, his son was greatly afraid of jumping into the deep ocean. His father spoke again, "I will give you to the count to five, and then you must jump from the mast. If not, then after I count to five, I will shoot you."

The son knew very well that his father was a man of his word. Then he thought to himself, "If I don't jump into the ocean, my father will shoot me and I will die." But when he thought about jumping, it seemed as if the dark blue ocean would swallow him up, and it made him afraid. He felt in his heart that even if he were to die, it would be better to die jumping into the ocean than getting shot. So when his father reached the count, "Three! Four!" his son kicked off the mast with all his strength and plunged into the ocean. Although he fell into the ocean, the sailors that were already down below quickly rescued the boy, and he survived.

While there was no way that anyone could have saved the son who was at the top of the mast, it was his father's wisdom that saved him. Because the son did not have that wisdom at the time, all he could do was hold tightly onto the mast. However, just because he holds tightly, does it mean that he will live? As time passes, he will lose more and more strength. Ultimately, when he cannot hold onto the mast any longer, he will fall onto the deck and die. His father yelled out to his son, "If you hold onto the mast, it seems as if you will live, but ultimately, you will die. You have to jump into the ocean before you lose any more of your strength!" That is what his father was telling his son. His son was so afraid that he would never have dared do that. For that reason, the father aimed the gun at his son and said, "Jump into the ocean, or I will shoot you." He did not give his son a choice. When the son followed his father's words and jumped into the ocean, only then was he able to live.

It is the same with our lives. The reason we live in difficulty and pain is because we are short on wisdom and we are lacking in thought. In such a time, it is not that we have to strengthen ourselves in order to do something. We must learn how to be freed from ourselves in order to accept the wisdom and thoughts that come from somewhere else. When you accept the wisdom that you could not have gained on your own, and if you receive the hope, peace, and joy of another person, your life can change.

Once You Acquire the Taste of Durian, It Doesn't Smell so Terrible Anymore

A long time ago when I went to Vietnam, I experienced something that I will never forget. It all started one evening when I was returning to my hotel room. I detected a foul odor. It was the same kind of foul odor I remembered from the outhouses of my youth. Without any further thought, I said to myself, "I guess they must be cleaning out the outhouses in the hotel today. But all the bathrooms of the hotel flushed on their own. When I entered my room, what shocked me was the fact that that the smell was actually coming from my room. When I located the source of the odor, there was a large fruit called durian on my table. The missionary's wife in Vietnam had taken that spiky fruit and cut it open with a knife and said, "Pastor, this fruit is very expensive, but is very delicious and good for your health. Please have some." The stench, however, nauseated me, so I did not want to eat it. "How could I eat such a smelly thing?" I asked myself. She urged me so sincerely that I could not refuse, so I simply put it in my mouth on it. "I guess it is a good fruit, but it does not fit my taste. I sincerely hope that I will not have to eat any more durian," I thought. After everything was finished in Vietnam, I went to Thailand. But in Thailand, they gave me durian as well. Then I traveled to Cambodia. They gave me durian once again. Even when I went to Myanmar, they said that durian was precious and gave me more of it. Therefore I had no choice but to have it once, then twice. As I continued to eat it over and over again, something amazing happened. It started to become more and more delicious. Do you know what the nickname for durian is? It is, "The Smell of Hell and the Taste of Heaven." The smell is quite foul, but it tastes very delicious.

When I was first introduced to durian, it had a smell from hell and the taste from hell. But as I kept eating it, I began to enjoy the true taste of durian more and more. "Durian tastes pretty good," I thought. The more I ate it, the better it became. After getting to know the flavor of durian, even the foul odor was no longer a problem at all. Of course it still smelled awful, but it was no longer as foul as it had been the first time. "Why did it only smell terrible when I first had it?" I thought to myself. From then on, I began to like durian. Whenever I visit countries in Southeast Asia, there are times when I purposely visit durian stores. The streets of Cambodia are filled with durian especially in the month of May.

As I ate durian, I learned something very interesting: people are similar to fruit. Fruits all have their own unique taste and flavors. Apples have their own flavor; peaches have their own flavor; and bananas have their own flavor, too. When you meet people, they are just like fruit. In the same way that every fruit has its own unique flavor, people also have their

own unique flavors. In the beginning, you do not clearly recognize that flavor, but when you meet that person once, then
twice, you can start to sense the flavor that is unique to that
person. No matter who we meet, the first thing we do is look
at that person's exterior. We look at their faces and say that
the person is either good looking or bad looking, and that
is the full extent of what we know about the person. But,
after we meet other people several more times, we begin to
feel, "This person is impatient. This person is calmer than he
looks." We come to know these things. However, when we
get to know the person a little deeper, we get to see their true
heart. Some fruits are delicious in the beginning, but later
on, we grow sick of them. There are some fruits that seem
disgusting in the beginning, but we are able get to know its
actual flavor from eating them.

Some people, in the beginning, appear to be very good
and kind, but later on, they turn out to be people who lie and
deceive you. There are other people who seem bitter and picky
when you first meet them, but when you enter deep into their
hearts, they are people who just have a deeper flavor. Before
you begin to know the "flavor" of someone, in the same way
that you complain that durian stinks when you taste it for the
first time. When you first meet someone, you may not start
off thinking too highly of that person. But at a certain point,
when you sense the true flavor of that person, you begin to
love and eventually miss that person. When they are away,
you find yourself missing that person. Then the feelings of
discomfort that you had with that person in the beginning

disappear. So when you deal with people, do not just deal with them out of formality or obligation. You must deal with them with your entire heart. That is because no matter who they may be, you have to feel that person's heart in order to properly sense the person's flavor.

You Have to Live Sensing
the Flavor of People

For us to properly sense the flavor of people, we must not only speak with our mouths—we must also say what is in our hearts. Then we must taste the heart of that other person. When you get to know the heart of another person, you come to understand the unique flavor of that person. It has been 40 years since I married my wife. During the time I lived with her, I began to see that my wife has a flavor that I cannot sense in anyone else. There's a flavor that only my wife has. My daughter has a flavor that is totally unique to her. My son possesses a flavor that belongs solely to him.

My son's son and his family live in New York, in the United States. My grandson once called me from America. "Grandpa, hurry up and come to New York. I miss you." I also miss my family. This is because there is a unique flavor that my family has. Just as you grow more and more accustomed to the taste of durian, when you get to know a person more and more and sense that person's flavor, you become unable to see that person's flaws and blemishes. The foul odor is no longer there. People say many things to judge and criticize others. "That person always changes his mind! That person thinks he's so great. That person's so foolish. That person makes no sense."

Do you know when people say these things? It is before they learn the flavor of that other person. When you are able to sense the flavor of that person, amazingly, your first impression of that person disappears. "Now I see why he's so impatient." Then you begin to understand them. Before, you simply argued with him saying, "Why did you get so frustrated in the first place?" However, once you get to know that person's flavor, you begin to fully understand him and say, "It makes sense that he got frustrated."

No matter who it may be, all children are lovable to their parents because they know much about the flavor of their children. When comes to people, the closer we are, the better able we are to go beyond superficial things and feel their hearts. When you are able to feel people's hearts, you begin to long for their *flavor*.

When I was traveling to Paraguay, I was scheduled for a two-hour layover in New York before boarding the plane to South America. My son came to the airport with my grandchildren while I was in New York for my layover. My 6-year-old grandson saw me and said, "Grandpa! I wanted you to sleep over, but why are you leaving today? Can't you leave tomorrow? Why are you coming and leaving without spending the night at our house? I spent many nights at your house in Korea, Grandpa." While I was on the airplane, for the entire flight to South America, I kept hearing his voice. That is a flavor that I can only feel and receive from my grandson.

If my son were to say, "Dad, I want you to sleep over," that would be so strange.

You meet people from the heart. Then, there is a flavor that you can feel only from that person. And when you learn that flavor, you begin to miss that person's heart. You begin to long for them. When you deal with people from their hearts, then you become surrounded with good people, people you long for, people you miss, people who you want to eat with, people you are happy to see, and people who are happy. As you live like this, you become surrounded with people you love, and the people around you become peaceful as well. On the other hand, if you do not meet people from your heart, but only meet them outwardly, they will only appear to have a foul odor and you will not like them, like when you first deal with durian. "Why is that person here again? I don't like you. Get out of here." That is how you will feel in your heart. If you live like that, then you will only be surrounded by people you do not like.

Honey, I Don't Want to Live like That Anymore, So Please Forgive Me

A female college student from our church came to me and said, "Pastor, my father has hired a lawyer and filed for divorce." She was telling me that for 20 years her parents did not get along. Her mother felt as if her husband did not care for the family, so they were using separate bedrooms. And recently, she stopped cooking for her husband. Although they were a couple living under the same roof, they lived as complete strangers. The husband could no longer bear to live that way, so he filed for divorce.

I thought, "When this couple gets divorced, where will their only daughter live?" So I said this to the college student, "Tell your mother to tell your father that she is sorry. Then tell her to treat her husband well. Because, if they get a divorce, it's only going to be she who gets damaged."

Afterwards, I called her mother, and said, "I have heard about you and your husband."

"Yes, it is true."

"What are you going to do?"

"I'm going to divorce him. I didn't like living with him in the first place, so this is a good thing."

"Have you ever been divorced before?"

"No, I haven't."

"That's why you want to get divorced. If you've been through a divorce, you'd never want to be divorced. Do you think divorce is a good thing?"

"Whether it's good or bad, I don't like him. I'm sick and tired of him."

"Don't say that. When your husband comes home tonight, tell him that you're sorry. Then tell him that you don't want to get divorced."

"I cannot do that."

"What do you mean, you can't do that? You cannot get divorced. Listen to what I'm telling you. When you go home, use the same bedroom as your husband and cook for him."

I then called her husband and said to him, "I heard that you filed for divorce."

"Yes, Pastor, I have."

"Why did you do that?"

"Why would I go as far as getting a divorce? Because my wife is so mean. If this is how I am treated at this age, it seems that if I get any older, my life will become even more pitiful. So, before I get any older, I want to get divorced."

"I have told your wife to tell you that she is sorry, and that this will not happen again. So don't get divorced."

The husband promised that he would do so and left. The next morning, I called the daughter and asked her, "Did your mother and father sleep in the same room last night?"

"No, they did not."

"Did your mother cook for your father before he went to work?"

"No, she didn't."

I then became very angry. I called her mother, and said, "Serve your husband well, why don't you? What's so good about getting a divorce? Serving your husband is much easier than getting a divorce!"

I scolded her and after listening to me for a while, she turned her heart around.

She said, "I'm very sorry. Starting from today, I will do as you say, and when my husband comes home, I'll treat him well."

"Yes, do that." The next day, I called the young girl again and asked her, "Did your mother and father sleep in the same room last night?"

"Yes, they did."

"Did your mother cook for your father this morning?"

"Yes, she did."

That day, when her husband came home from work, the wife told him that she needed to tell him something.

"What is it that you want to say?"

"Honey, there are many bad things I've done to you during our time together."

The husband began to question what he was hearing. His wife would usually nag at him and scold him for his wrong-doings. He never once heard from his wife's lips that she was sorry.

He replied, "There's something I want to tell you as well. A few years ago, when my parents came here from the countryside, do you know how much you embarrassed me in front of them? I just sat there because I couldn't yell at you in front of my parents, but it was like hell. What would my mother and father think of us? And when my friends came over to our house, do you remember how you insulted me in front of them? Right then, I just wanted to die."

His wife had only remembered her husband's wrongdoings; she never thought of her own wrongdoings at all. Only when she heard her husband's words did she know that her husband was filled with bitterness and rage. "What a terrible woman I have been," she thought. For twenty years, her husband never once said a thing to her, but he had now brought out everything that was bottled up in his heart. Only then did his wife finally discover herself, and realize how wrong she was.

"Honey, I really had no idea that you felt this way. Why didn't you tell me about this earlier?"

"When we fight, have you ever given me a chance to talk? You just blast away at me as if you are firing off a machine gun. You are always right, and I have always been the one who was wrong. Have you ever *really* wanted to listen to me?"

His wife could not deny the fact that she had lived despising her husband. She truly felt that she was wrong. She knelt in front of her husband, and said, "Honey, I was so ignorant. I was terribly wrong. I cannot guarantee it will not happen again, but I will try. Please, forgive me." As her husband he saw his wife kneeling down and begging for forgiveness, his heart of bitterness completely melted away. "I haven't done so well myself. I have also done many wrong things. But from now on, let's live peacefully with one another." This couple that wanted to get divorced, finally, became one in heart.

People Must Have Their Hearts Flow into One Another

What was wrong with this couple? The wife nagged at her husband, thinking only about his mistakes. She never once considered her husband's position. But then the husband began to tell her the things that he had not been able to reveal for the past 20 years. Before, his wife would have interrupted her husband and fought him, but that day, for the first time, she listened to everything he had to say. After listening to everything, she realized how wrong she truly was.

Afterwards, the husband said to his wife, "Honey, I'm going on a business trip to Jeju Island today. I can finish my work for the company in just a few hours, so I want you to come with me. Let's take a few days off and tour the area." Since their honeymoon, it was the first time they were happily going on a trip together. Their daughter was so happy to see this.

People's hearts must flow into one another. Problems arise when people only accept their own thoughts and reject the thoughts of others. Because the hearts of the husband and his wife did not flow into each other, they tried to get a divorce. However, when their hearts flowed, they transformed into a happy couple. Just as fruits have different flavors; people have different flavors, too. No matter who a person may be, once that person deals with others from the heart, he can sense their flavors. Then when he senses their flavors, he can understand their actions. Then they are able to have the same flow of the heart. From then on, people begin to long for one another, and they actually desire to do something for the other person. Their hearts become filled with love and they become happy.

Chapter 10

Conversation

Don't Just Avoid Something because It Is Burdensome. Speak Your Heart with Your Father.

Whether it is politics or business, in order to succeed, you must gain the hearts of others. Opening one's heart is not like a math equation or provisions of the law that you have to memorize or know much of. While having a conversation, the heart opens and the thoughts automatically change.

The Performer Who Believes You Must Become One-Hearted with the Piano to Perform Well

It does not take something grand to change your life. Rather, change of the heart begins from small things. Until now we have discussed the shape of the heart and the way the heart flows. Now let us not just remain in our thoughts, and let us not see this as mere knowledge. We are now at the stage of saying what is in our hearts to one another. You may be worried or afraid to share what's in your heart, but actually, it is okay. The hearts of people are pretty much the same as everyone else's.

I went to Russia and got to know many famous musicians. There I met a pianist named Izabella. She believes the piano is alive; therefore, it is not she who plays the piano. She has said that her heart has to flow with the piano in order for it to make a good sound.

We often invite famous people and listen to their lectures during the World Camp. Once we invited a mountaineer, Mr. Hong Gil Uhm, who had climbed the 16 highest peaks on Earth. We've also invited one of the actual survivors portrayed in the movie, "Alive," who survived after his plane crashed in the Andes Mountains by eating the dead bodies of his deceased colleagues. We found that the common ground they shared in their lectures was that they both shared their hearts with the mountain.

Just as the pianist Izabella shared her heart with the piano for a mutual response from the piano, when we share our hearts with another person, we become one. Because the heart cannot flow, we are unable to understand the heart. People only try to control actions on the surface. If a son has fallen into video games while on a riotous path, then his parents will do whatever it takes to try and stop him. However, this method will not work out. Suppose a river does not flow to the ocean. If you dig a waterway to the ocean, then the river will automatically flow into it. On the other hand, if you try to scoop the water and pour it into the ocean, think of how difficult that would be. What do you do during the rainy season when your yard is filled with rainwater? If you just unclog the sewer drainage, then the water will naturally flow out.

The world of the heart is no different. When people's hearts automatically flow into other people's hearts, they become comfortable and the things that are wrong are automatically cleansed. But because people do not understand this, they try to scoop up water and force it into the ocean. No matter how pretty your face may be, no matter how much money you may have, no matter how smart you may be, if you have a defect in your heart, then you become tormented and you bring lots of pain to the people around you. In light of all this, it is better to be a person who has physical disabilities with a healthy heart, than to be a person who has disabilities of the heart. In reality, they are the ones whose problems are the most serious.

But people do not really know why they have "disabilities of the heart", and even worse, they do not know how to treat these disabilities. Trying to stop from gambling, drinking, playing computer games, taking drugs, or having sexual encounters, has made people extremely stressed out as they try to stop their bad behavior. Among the people who have fallen into drugs and computer games, none of them ever started because they wanted to end up the way that they did. At first, they only started doing these things for fun, but as they fell deeper and deeper into these things, they grew even more determined to break free. Nevertheless, they ended up being dragged into it more and more. Trying to advise such a person to stop doing what he or she is doing is not helpful in any way. If you know about the world of the heart, you can easily take care of these problems. The first thing to do is to open your heart. When you listen closely to what other people are saying, don't just listen to their stories—open the ears of your heart to hear what they are *really* saying. You must listen to what they are saying with the voice of their heart and turn them into people that you can share your heart with through that. You will suddenly be filled with energy in your life, and you will become joyful.

We are made to live belonging to this society. You can never live normally by yourself. The Lord, the Creator, made the hearts of men. So when we receive the love of the Lord, our Creator into our hearts, then thankfulness automatically flows into our hearts. We have been programmed to be able to feel His love. We are also able to enjoy peace in our hearts. Although we can see a person's face, we cannot see his or her heart. Without self-expression through language, it is difficult to know the heart of another. Isn't language the tool that was made to express the heart? Even if you are busy, do not just speak about the things that are related to your job, and do not have only superficial conversations. "I'm so worried today. I'm so happy today. I am in difficulty because these problems. This really concerns me." Please speak about the condition of your heart regarding these things.

In a few years, people who are college students now will get married. At that time, it is important to reveal everything in your heart to the person who will be your husband or wife. Do not hide, cover, or leave anything out. You should say whatever is in your heart, exactly as it is to your spouse. Talk about how you are sad today. Talk about how your heart is happy and the reasons why. Mention how you felt in your heart when you acted in a certain way. When two people share what is in their hearts in this way, then the husband is able to know what is inside his wife's heart, and the wife gets to learn what is inside her husband's heart. Once the husband knows his wife's heart, he is able to feel her heart and trust her. When the two of them are truly able to trust one another, it is then and only then that rest comes upon their hearts. How uncomfortable would it be if a phone could neither make nor receive calls at the same time? It would be a problem if the phone could only receive calls, and it would also be a problem if the phone could only make calls. In the same way, the heart has to be able to communicate both ways. Then the heart can receive joy and strength, and experience amazing things. When you have someone to share your heart with, you can trust in each other's hearts. Then no matter what problems you may face, those problems will not remain as problems; they will get taken care of. I experienced this many times in my life. Our young people need to change from living a life of being isolated with a closed heart, to living their lives opening their hearts. But first of all, speak about the things of your heart with your father.

Father, Do You Think You Can Live with a Mistress Even When You Are Old? Be Good to Mother Now

There is a missionary I know who was very scared of his father when he was a college student. Even though he had already graduated from graduate school, he was always afraid of his father. He was always afraid to be around him. One day, right before he went overseas as a missionary, he told me all about his worries. He told me that when he goes abroad, he would not be able to care for his mother. He told me that he had been tormented for a long time, seeing his father living with a different woman and mistreating his mother. I told him to go to his father and tell him exactly what I said.

"What should I say to him?" he asked.

Tell him, "Father, I'm going overseas as a missionary. I came here because there is something that I wanted to tell you. When I see the people of this world, when they are young, they have fun with their mistresses, but when they get older, they all return to their true wives. Father, you are no exception. You can have a mistress when you are young, but not when you are old. The time will come when you will want to eat from Mother's table. That means that you will need to provide some money for Mother. You must provide her a home to stay in and a monthly allowance. Who will become the head of the family when you pass away, Father? I will. Father, when you get old and become ill, you will have no one else but your son. So provide me with enough now so that I can support you when you become old. You are healthy now, Father, but you will not always be young."

How was this missionary supposed to speak to his father this way when he was so scared? I told him to memorize what I said and repeat it to his father. He finally went to his father and said, "Father, I have come here because there is something that I want to tell you." He then began to speak, but his heart was literally pounding. He started to recite everything that he had memorized. And without him even knowing it, all these other things began to come out from his heart. He thought his father would respond, "Why you little punk!" and would come after him with a stick. On the contrary, with a look of amazement, his father said to him, "Son, have you thought that deeply about my future? I am so fortunate to have a son who worries about me. I will now put everything else aside and come home before I get any older."

The missionary's father was so touched by his son's proposal that from then on, the way that he looked at his son completely changed. And just as his son had asked, he provided his mother with a house, paid for her living expenses, and gave some money to his son as well. Whether sons say good things or bad things, fathers fundamentally love their children. There may be people who would deny this, but they say this because they do not see the inner heart of their fathers. If you have not done so already, say what is in your heart to your father. "Father, this is how I feel in my heart. Teach me if I'm wrong. Father, I was disappointed about this. Father, why didn't you do this for me? Father, I was thankful for these things. I love you, Father." Please go and speak to your father. Are there people out there who are so burdened about speaking to their fathers and looking into their faces that they just simply hang their heads when they see them? Korean fathers, who appear to always be solemn and too shy to express their hearts, may seem to be cold and apathetic to their children. But fathers were made to love their children. And even though it may seem they are not listening and that they do not care, fathers are able to accept almost anything you say.

After that, go to the person who you have the most difficulty sharing your heart with. Say what is in your heart. "Uncle, older brother, upper classman, these are the kinds of thoughts I've had." Your father has to know your heart. Your mother has to know your heart. Your uncle has to know your heart. Your older brother has to know your heart. Your elders have to know your heart. Older brothers must also speak to their younger brothers, and say, "This is the heart that I have." "This is what I like about you." The older brother must also say what is in his heart often. Then, when the younger brother's heart flows together with his older brother's heart, their relationship will change.

Do not wait for the other person to open his heart first. When you open your heart to the other person first and say what is in your heart once, twice, three times, and four times, your heart changes. There is one bad thing about young college students these days. They try to avoid whatever is burdensome. In fact, they do not even consider trying. Whatever they do not like, they just reject unconditionally. But there are times, when you have to do burdensome things as you live your life, and you have to meet people you do not like. You probably already know this, but there are times when you have to refrain from doing things you really want to do.

Just because the Water Is Your Enemy, Can You Live without Drinking Water?

A few years ago, there was an American student from Florida, named, Jennifer, who attended the World Camp in Korea. She majored in psychology. As the camp was drawing to a close, many students were changing, but Jennifer closed her heart and avoided any conversation.

Her teacher came to her and asked, "Jennifer, why is your heart like a rock?"

"Teacher, why are you trying to pick at a rock with a toothpick?

Will it make a hole in the rock?

Just leave me alone. I like living the way I live."

Among the ten students in her class, nine of them had changed, but Jennifer was not able to fit into the flow. Three days before the closing of the camp, her teacher came to see me. She said, "Pastor, please meet with Jennifer from my class. She is determined to close her heart to the very end. It is extremely saddening."

So I met with Jennifer and her teacher. First, it was the teacher who began to speak.

"Jennifer, can't you open your heart just a little bit?"

"I'm never going to open my heart no matter what you say, Teacher."

Then I began to talk. "It is your choice whether you open your heart or not. If you don't want to open your heart, then I guess that's it. It's your choice if you'd like to open your heart, or if you'd like to keep it closed forever. But why don't you want to open your heart? I want to hear your reason for that. Surely, there is a reason that you've chosen not to open your heart. I'd like to hear that reason. Could you at least tell me that much?"

At first, Jennifer hesitated, but she finally opened her mouth. There was an older guy at the church that she attended in Florida. Since he had an outgoing personality and was honest, everyone considered him to be a pillar of the church. Jennifer followed him sincerely and he was five years older. One day she was raped by that young man. She was so disheartened by this; she went to her pastor and told him about it. The pastor immediately called that young man and confronted him.

"Why have you done this to Jennifer?"

"Pastor, I didn't do anything. She is the one who was always following me around every day. But, because I did not care for her in that way, she is making things up that never happened. She is conspiring against me." This young man completely lied, but because he was seen as such an honest person all the time, the pastor of the church chose to believe him.

"How could this happen? How could this be?" she thought. Even greater than the shame and bitterness of having been raped, she felt so wronged and enraged about the fact that nobody would listen to what she had to say. Then Jennifer came to the conclusion, "What was wrong with me that I followed that young man around? I was so foolish to open my heart to him!" Then she cried endlessly. In the end, she made a vow in her heart: "From now on, I will never open my heart to anyone! From now on, I am only going to keep to myself and live by myself. It was my fault for trusting someone else. That is why I have become so miserable." Afterwards, Jennifer never opened her heart to anyone else. And although she was attending the World Camp, she had already locked her heart tightly away. Other students were having a great time, but she remained all by herself.

After she told me her story, I replied with these words: "I can completely understand the sadness and disappointment you have in your heart because of what you have experienced. I can also see that the shock of what has happened to you has kept you from opening your heart. But that is wrong. Suppose there was a fire and your house was completely burned down. If the violin that you cherished the most in this world also burned up, then you would think that fire is your enemy. But, does that mean that you can live without fire? You have to use fire to cook food. You need fire to heat the water you shower with. It is true that fire became your enemy, but when you need to use it, you have to use it.

"Then suppose there was a flood, and your house was swept away. Suppose everyone you loved drowned in the flood. Then you'd consider floods to be your enemy, and you would no longer like water at all. Regardless of this, does that mean that you can live without drinking water? You can't do that. Jennifer, it truly saddens me that you had to go through that misery and pain. However, when it is time for you to open your heart, you have to open your heart. It is foolish to close your heart forever just because you were hurt before."

I then spoke to her about a story in the Bible. Jennifer then asked me, "Pastor, why do you only talk about the Bible?"

So I answered, "When you go to a music school, all they teach is music. Nobody ever says anything about that. When you go to art school, they only teach art, and yet nobody questions the reason they don't teach music. I have discovered the solutions to the problems that college students like you face within the Bible. Through the Bible, I was able to truly identify the problems, and teach the actual solutions to them. I have not discovered a book that is better at treating the wounds of the heart. And actually, the stories in this book have changed my life as well."

That day, Jennifer finally opened her heart and the rage she had against the world began to disappear. From that moment on, Jennifer drastically changed into a bright, happy student.

We must no longer hide from our burdens. We need to train ourselves to go beyond them. The first step to accomplishing this is to open our hearts. Then we need to reveal our hearts to others. If we do this, it seems as if it will result in great losses, but in actuality, you will be able to make true friends. When you are in pain, when you are exhausted, and when you are in great difficulty, the most important thing is to have a friend to who will stand by you with whom you can share your heart. I'm not talking about having friends to go drinking with, or friends to go out with to have fun. You need friends who you can unite your heart with.

When you are done through reading this book, tell your friends the things you have hidden in your heart. When you actually say what is in your heart, you may become afraid that your friends will leave you. Even so, go ahead and try it. While you are at it, go ahead and reveal all the shameful things that you have not been unable to tell anyone, the mistakes that you have made against other people, and all the other things you have hidden away. Express your heart to your friends. And when your friends say what is in their hearts in return, accept everything exactly as they say it.

People today are busy dealing with large numbers of people, but since their hearts are empty and lonely, they need true friends with whom they can really share their hearts. Have you ever really poured out what is in your heart to a close friend? When you open your heart, you gain so much peace and your thoughts become much healthier. In addition, you become very progressive and wise. As a result, your life begins to change at a very fast pace.

No matter what it is you do, do it with all your heart. The same way electricity flows when the negative tip and positive tip are connected, when our hearts become one with another person's heart, we can take care of any problem. Even when you start a business, do not do it by yourself. You have to meet with other people and gain their hearts in order to complete the work. Even when you are running for office, it is only possible to gain votes when you gain people's hearts. That is why when young college students decide to do something, the most important thing is that they understand the other person's heart, and then gain that person's heart.

To succeed in this world, you need to nurture your English skills, have a lot of specialized knowledge, and many different licenses. However, what the world needs the most today are people with open hearts. When you meet people who are doing well in the world, they are very capable and smart. If you speak with them, you will see that they are so "rich" in specialized knowledge that no one can keep up with them. However, there are many people who do not know about the world of the heart at all, and there are also people who cannot understand what opening their heart means. Opening your heart is not a mathematical principle or a law. It is not memorizing something, doing lots of things or knowing a lot. People will automatically change if they open their hearts. This is what will turn young people into great people, and will lead them to become individuals who could never be any happier.

Due to financial difficulties, my dream of becoming a photographer shattered so I threw myself into alcohol and cigarettes. I needed a change so I headed to Togo. The country seemed dirty and poor, and the first meal there was gumbo sauce and adme sauce that resembled a mixture of snot and phlegm. I couldn't even touch it. My one year in Africa, where I never thought I could feel close, I got to know the people's hearts of always wanting to give. Later I even wished I was African. Africa made me into one of the Togolese... I still cannot forget the gumbo sauce and adme sauce that I shared with them.

Hye Mee Kim (Good New Corps
Overseas Volunteer to Togo)

People of India who, unlike their particularly rough hands, have soft and warm hearts. In Orissa, where people of lowest class live, although they cannot get out of the bondage of slavery, they surrender to their fate. People who quietly accepted me, selfish and self-centered... They who still liked me, their eyes with peace and joy even in their difficult daily lives, are fresh in my memory.

Seo In Cho (Good News Corps
Overseas Volunteer to India)

I believed that money would bring me happiness but the more money I made, my desire was not satisfied and because I couldn't trust anyone, my life became exhausting. I met people in Congo who thought of my matters as their own when I became sick or sad, and I got to know that true happiness is not in money but in the heart. Also, I got to discover the love of my parents that was overshadowed by poverty that I couldn't see before.

Kee Dong Yoon (Good News Corps Overseas Volunteer to the Republic of Congo, far left)

In our family, we had a motto: "Be someone who is indispensable." But as a member of a gang since middle school, I was a social evil that brought harm to others. Having wanted to travel away to some place, I came to Nepal to volunteer and for the first time became someone indispensable to somebody else. Even though I could not speak Nepalese well, people welcomed me with warm hearts. I shared that love through Taekwondo. In this place that is said to be without vision, I found a new hope.

Sang Hun Choi (Good News Corps
Overseas Volunteer to Nepal,
second from left)

From a young age, because I helped with my father's laborious farming work, my clothes were dirty and smelled like sweat, so school friends isolated me. If I were to reveal what was inside of me, I thought I'd be rejected so I lived hiding them. I went overseas to do volunteer work in the Czech Republic, and the people showed much interest to me who was Asian. One day I was talking about my difficult past and realized that I was receiving interest and love from many Czech friends. I'm thankful to that love, so I want to live for Czech people.

Young Hwa Kim (Good News Corps
Overseas Volunteer to the Czech Republic)

I grew up in a wealthy family doing whatever I wanted. Brand-name clothing, the latest gizmos, everything I wanted, parties, alcohol, and many girlfriends, but my heart was empty. I somehow ended up in Togo. Burning hot weather of 40 degrees Celsius, unpaved roads filled with trash and different animals running around on top of them... I only complained about Africa. During my no-money witnessing trip, as I saw those pure people who accepted me and black friends who took care of me all night when I was sick, I realized how happy it is to live for others.

Bum Kyoo Seo (Good News Corps
Overseas Volunteer to Togo)

I thought that I couldn't live freely because of my strict father so I began to express myself rebelliously since college. However, as I met a 12-year-old girl in Mexico with three children of her own with different fathers, I realized that the fence of my father, which I so hated before, was something very precious and safe.

Ryun Choi (Good News Corps
Overseas Volunteer to Mexico,
far right)

The day I put a tea leaf basket on my head in Haddigal village, at an unexpected pace, I hurried my hand-movements but made more mistakes. As we breathed in the scent of grass, the laughter was endless; to me who grew up without hardships, those times taught me the joy of labor. For the year, as I shared friend-ships with people of India and tried difficult works, I who used to be called a faucet because I cried so easily, became mature.

Mee Hyung Kim (Good News Corps
Overseas Volunteer to India,
third from the left)

I was so introverted and impatient that many times I would give up. However, as I did burdensome work in Ukraine, such as enduring the cold weather, learning the difficult language, and inviting famous people to various events, I became a strong person. Now, I have no limit.

Eun Young Lee (Good News Corps
Overseas Volunteer to Ukraine)

I am a typical man of Gyeongsang Province. In Poland, where I volunteered, because Koreans were rare and the language was different, I became an even quieter person. Then one day, I got closer to a friend called Kuba and learned Polish. Kuba made me understand Poland to be a friendly country, and changed me-a man of Gyeongsang Province-to be like a little child, talkative and cheerful.

Yong Soo Kim (Good News Corps
Overseas Volunteer to Poland)

I hated my mother's constant interference, so I grew up as a rebel. Then, as I collided with other volunteers in Zambia and the people, I discovered that I only insist on my thoughts. I thought I was always right. Was I really a decent person? I realized that I, who despised everyone, was the worst person. I got to know that there was love and care hidden inside my mother's nagging that I hated so much.

Joon Pil Hwang (Good News Corps
Overseas Voluteer to Zambia, center)

Under the hot sunlight without a trace of a cloud, I met many Africans. When I spoke in broken English, they understood me exactly and translated into their native language. We would drive through unpaved roads in a jeep for hours; it is something that I'd never have experienced if I stayed in Korea.

Minju Jee (Good News Corps
Overseas Volunteer to Kenya,
back row, left of the picture)

I was admitted into medical school, thinking of the value of saving lives. However, from the first day, due to forced drinking and images of selfish medical students, my dream was shattered. Then, in order to keep the promise with Dudu whom I met during the World Camp, I went to South Africa as an overseas volunteer, and there I heard shocking news that she died of AIDS. From then on, I took each moment preciously, took care of people there, and experienced how their pain and their joy became my own. Africa made me the happiest doctor in the world. Even now when I recollect my memory of Africa, there is a smile on my face.

So Young Park (Good News Corps
Overseas Volunteer to South Africa)

I was born in North Korea and successfully escaped with my father, risking our lives, however, in South Korea where you have to decide your own life, our lives were overwhelming. Needing a new escape, I left to Tanzania, and I saw the people who would freely come to me and talk to me and play around. I saw myself as someone who couldn't open my heart to anyone because I lived under a surveillance system for so long. At my story, they cried as if it were their own, and comforted me; they taught me how a person's heart meets another. Africa let me know how happy it is to encounter people, and there, I gained true freedom.

Dong Woo Han (Good News Corps
Overseas Volunteer to Tanzania,
left, center of the picture)

I believed that having no problems with people and laughing energetically was all I needed. Everyone liked me and I thought of myself as a decent person. In Benin, where I went as an overseas volunteer, I had the heart to despise the native culture and the people, which were below my standards. Unlike me, people of Benin easily acknowledged and accepted their own wrongdoings. As I saw their purity, I realized how arrogant I was.

Eun Hye Kim (Good News Corps
Overseas Volunteer to Benin)

I was born in a wealthy family and lived without lacking much, but because my younger brother who was the only son of the family hogged my parents' love, I comforted my loneliness with drinking and friends. Due to a stomach disorder, I couldn't even drink anymore and thought of suicide. That was when I heard about the overseas volunteer program and left for Cameroon. There I heard the news that my brother who used to be healthy, collapsed with arrhythmia; I got to see how selfish I had been under a victim's mentality. I also got to know the love of my host family and friends towards me, in spite of who I am. The fact that I discovered such immense love made me a truly happy person.

Bo Min Kim (Good News Corps
Overseas Volunteer to Cameroon)

I always thought of myself as an unfortunate kid who was not loved by her parents. One day, in Tanzania, Africa where I went as an overseas volunteer, my friend Ramson invited me to his hometown, Lindy. It's a place where there's no food and such dirty water that even Tanzanians are reluctant to go there. But we were able to feel the love of Ramson's family through just one bucket of water and a plate of simple food. Meanwhile, I was able to discover my mother's devoted love towards me. Poverty in Lindy village opened the eyes of my heart.

Da Hye Kim (Good News Corps
Overseas Volunteer to Tanzania far left)

I was never able to do hard labor, yet I often had to walk up a high mountain in Nepal. My face would turn red and my whole body got wet with sweat but I learned many things on the mountain. Difficulties made me strong and the children growing up brightly in the mountain made my heart also pure.

Jinok Yoon (Good News Corps
Overseas Volunteer to Nepal)

Due to my parents' constant quarrels, I used to cry often but changed into a person who covers up the sadness with a happy face. During overseas volunteer work in Peru, I gave a piece of cookie to a poor kid from the family of an unwed mother, and he gave half the piece back to me. Even an impoverished kid has a warm heart! My cold heart started to melt. The day I parted with those who stirred up my emotion, we held each other and cried so much.

Ji Hye Jung (Good News Corps
Overseas Volunteer to Peru)

Due to my difficult family circumstances and the fact that we moved often, I couldn't make friends well during my school years. In addition, my parents opposed my dream of becoming a cartoonist; I hated all of those things. However, as I saw the people of Myanmar who, if they have kids when they are poor, throw them away or make them work, I realized how childish I have been. How thankful is it just to be able to do volunteer works with a healthy body? Now I have a dream: it is to live for the people of Myanmar who taught me thankfulness.

Jong Eun Jang (Good News Corps
Overseas Volunteer to Myanmar)

Due to my parents' sudden divorce, I was shocked and left for Ghana, Africa. I lived with Charles' family there and I often panicked from constant mistakes. Unlike me, Charles' wife, Cynthia, was very accepting of my weaknesses. "Because we are family, the more mistakes you make, the closer we become." They were not educated or wealthy, but African families taught me how to open my heart and become free with people. I miss my family in Africa.

Hanna Jang (Good News Corps
Overseas Volunteer to Ghana)

I used to blame my father, thinking that my life was ruined because of him. However, in Chile, I saw myself who was selfish and foolish, who couldn't even control my appetite and could only collide with others, and realized that I was the one ruining my own life. I got to know myself amongst Chileans, as I did volunteer work. I got to learn a new heart.

Mee Hyun Lim (Good News Corps
Overseas Volunteer to Chile)

I thought I had to do everything well for people to like me. However, Africans accepted me and loved me even when I made mistakes and did wrong. They freed me from my complexes and timidness.

Dongi Jung (Good News Corps
Overseas Volunteer to Ivory Coast)

I thought I was unfortunate because of poverty and an unpleasant family, however, the people I met in Colombia were different from me. In an environment more difficult than mine, they bestowed love and were happy. I had the heart that I was unfortunate, that was why I was unfortunate. As I met Colombians who had great happiness, their happiness caught onto me.

Jina Park (Good News Corps
Overseas Volunteer to Colombia)

We went on moneyless witnessing trip to a place called "Parapenni". However, because it was rainy season, all of sudden it started pouring, and the street, in moments, became a small stream. I didn't want to ruin my one and only pair of shoes so I put my belly against the wall to pass through; it was so funny! Just as the little stream created an unforgettable memory, poverty and difficulties in Gambia weaved us closer and gave us the heart to be thankful for even small things, and be there for one another. It was the unforgettable time of my life that I would have never tasted if I stayed in Korea where everything is set.

Shee Eun Kim (Good News Corps
Overseas Volunteer to Gambia)

Deep in the wilds of the Amazon, Indio kids are growing up in an environment away from the privilege of civilization. As I saw those children, I was very ashamed of myself for not being thankful and for venting all the time even though I had so many things to enjoy in Korea. And, I wanted to share many things I had with these children.

Jung Hee Shin (Good News Corps
Overseas Volunteer to Brazil)

The day I drew water from the well with a bucket for the first time in my life, somehow I scooped up some water from the well but I was frantic because I couldn't pull it up. Then an Indian woman offered a kind hand. A Korean proverb said, "two heads are better than one." With her help, drawing well water became something fun. I used to only care about myself, but the memory that taught me the joy of sharing still remains in my heart.

Hye Mee Shin (Good News Corps
Overseas Volunteer to India)

As my family situation fell apart, I worked at bars and went on the wrong path. All I had left was emptiness, but I saw my older sister change after participating in the overseas volunteer program, I too left for Ghana. Although many were dying because they didn't have one dollar to buy malaria medicine, they still gave what little they had to others. Friends who lived brightly even in difficult situations, brought me great strength. I couldn't get out of darkness yet they embraced me and led me, so now, I get to dream.

Tae Hyun Uhm (Good News Corps
Overseas Volunteer to Ghana)

People work hard under the sun all day to make 20-30 cents, and starving children go out to streets grabbing their stomachs to make money. It is hard to provide one meal, yet still with bright faces they greet each other and do not simply pass by their neighbors' pain even if their own lives are difficult. Nobody resents or complains about his or her own circumstances. In Liberia, where I thought no happiness could be found, I realized that happiness does not lie in material things but in the warmth of the heart.

Hanna Lee (Good News Corps
Overseas Volunteer to Liberia)

Tall trees laden with fully ripe "aguacate." No matter
how much I swing my stick at it, it doesn't even budge.
My local friend who had been watching silently
behind me swings his stick, at which the fruits fall
to the ground. At that moment, the pride I had in
myself, thinking I was good, all fell away. Paraguay is
one of the poorest nations in the world. As much as
the weather is fickle, the people are naïve. "Exchange
your youth for their hearts." I had been long forget-
ting what I was to live for. The "aguacate" that my
friend and I bit into was sweeter and more refreshing
than ever before.

Jong Hwi Yoo (Good News Corps
Overseas Volunteer to Paraguay)

I wanted to be freed from video games. I left to Tanzania as an escape and there, African friends welcomed me by thanking me for coming to their country. The blue sea that resembled them, as we played on the white sand, for the first time I started to like being with people. Tanzania, the place that freed me from games and the heart of being trapped alone... I can never forget that place.

Hyung Kun Choi (Good News Corps
Overseas Volunteer to Tanzania)

Volunteering abroad was the turning point of my life. When I recall that year, riddled with countless mistakes and blunders that occurred every day, my face gets flushed. That experience of discovering how infinitely small I was became a source of strength for me in trying to newly discipline myself after I came back to Korea. I was always alone, but I am truly grateful for those times that taught me how to live with someone. (I took the photo with children in the remote area of "Chaco.")

Min Ju Kang (Good News Corps Overseas Volunteer to Paraguay)

Bio

The author, Pastor Ock Soo Park, was born in 1944 in Seonsan, Gyeongbuk Province, in South Korea. In 1962, he received the grace of being born again and became a pastor. Since then, for over fifty years, he has dedicated his efforts to spreading the gospel. His meeting with a young Korean-American named Andy in 1993 began his interest in youth problems, and in 2001, he founded the International Youth Fellowship. Every year, he delivers mind lectures about the world of the heart to young people all over the world.